Perspectives on Social Problems
Second Edition

CANADIAN SOCIAL PROBLEMS SERIES

GENERAL EDITOR
Anne-Marie Ambert
YORK UNIVERSITY

Perspectives on Social Problems
Second Edition

Richard L. Henshel
Anne-Marie Henshel

ACADEMIC PRESS CANADA

Copyright © 1973, 1983 by Academic Press Canada
55 Barber Greene Road, Don Mills, Ontario M3C 2A1

ISBN 0-7747-3041-2

5 4 3 2 1   83 84 85 86 87

Printed in Canada
Composition by CompuScreen Typesetting Ltd.

Contents

Acknowledgments

It is as appropriate now as it was on the publication of the First Edition of this book to acknowledge the many people whose work has guided and clarified our thinking. Much of this indebtedness is openly stated in the footnotes to each chapter. Some of it no doubt goes unacknowledged precisely because it is pervasive.

We are particularly grateful to those of our colleagues who read and commented upon the manuscript for the First Edition: Orrin Klapp, John Kunkel, Allan McDougall, Raymond Morris, Anthony Richmond, James Rinehart, Ian Rockett, Robert Silverman, and Mark Wexler. Our thanks go also to those assistants who eased the burden of research and manuscript preparation: Gloria Cohen, Jean Liebman, Teresa Stott and Helen Trew.

While every effort has been made to acknowledge copyright in the footnotes, all errors or omissions, if called to our attention, will be corrected in future printings.

Preface to the Second Edition

In the preparation of this Second Edition, some sections have been greatly reworked. Chapter 1 includes for the first time material on psychological ethics and allied efforts to surmount the difficulties of cultural relativism. In Chapter 3, there has been a major effort to reflect the current research and controversy respecting the labeling perspective. Chapter 4 is one of the most reworked; the section on the mass media has been greatly expanded to take in the issues of concentration of ownership, agenda setting, event velocity, the manufacture of news, bureaucratic propaganda, and institutional advertising. Chapter 5 now covers the distinction between crimes *mala in se* and *mala prohibita*, and applies this to victimless crime. It also looks for the first time at the interconnections of the state and organized religion in defining social problems, and at the links between religion and egalitarian movements, via the "social gospel." Chapter 6 is completely restructured. Included for the first time are discussions of the growth of the knowledge industry and the power this is said to convey, the empirical issues this raises, formal education as occupational selection, the significance of peer group censure for writers and scholars, the temptations of grantsmanship, and the influence of institutional pressures at the University and the research institute. Chapter 7 now includes a discussion of the effects of political affiliation on police discretion, Rosenhan's study of the "stickiness" of mental labels once applied, and an expansion of the existing discussion of Lifton's notion of totalist therapy. Finally, Chapter 8 has been doubled in size to provide an overview of the central themes of the preceding seven chapters.

Readers familiar with the First Edition will find that other sections of the text have also been substantially improved through the updating of references, an increase in the number of Canadian citations, the inclusion of entirely new passages, and the reworking of paragraphs. A principal concern throughout has been to clarify difficult passages and provide more current illustrations. The Second Edition also boasts a significantly improved index, which should be of use to students and scholars alike. Together with the Glossary and References sections, the new index should be helpful for classroom use. The Preface to the Series (pages xi to xiv following) has been left unrevised, for purposes of historical comparison. It is gratifying to point out, though, that many of the research deficiencies it mentions are no longer with us.

It is our hope that the gratifying response accorded to the First Edition for ten years will be repeated for a new generation of students and scholars.

February, 1983   R.L.H. and A.-M. H.

Preface to the Series (1973)

PERSPECTIVES ON SOCIAL PROBLEMS is the first volume in a series of monographs on social problems in Canadian society. While this book is theoretical and general, each subsequent monograph in the series will be devoted to a particular set of deleterious social conditions such as poverty or social inequality, unemployment, inter-group tensions, crime, health care, mental illness, and sex roles. As time passes, the list will expand. We expect that several of our forthcoming monographs will be outdated within the decade as social conditions evolve and as research data accumulate on any subject; therefore, topical monographs will be re-edited and updated to follow these trends. The series will consequently offer a well-rounded perspective on social problems insofar as sociology has made sufficient inroads on the various topics covered.

The obstacles in the planning of such a series at this point are manifold. For one, there is presently a tremendous demand on the part of the educated public, especially within the universities, for Canadian material.[1] This situation may lead scholars to publish under pressure and neglect fundamental issues. Concern for output rather than meticulous research on any given area becomes a problem of paramount importance to a series with a long-range perspective, attempting to reach beyond mere consumerism.

Exacerbating this difficulty is the fact that our "national" sociology suffers from numerous gaps, both theoretically and

---

1. See the various discussions on this and related topics in *The Struggle for Canadian Universities*, by Robin Mathews and James Steele, Toronto: New Press, 1970.

empirically. This lacuna is especially evident in the field of social problems. For instance, a survey carried out in 1967 by Connor and Curtis revealed a relatively low level of interest by Canadian sociologists in all areas related to social problems.[2] In fact, there were few Canadian sociologists who could mention social problems as a major interest in terms of research and teaching time devoted to that area. In spite of some encouraging developments in the past few years, we are still affected by the long-range consequences of past uninterest in social problems.

Although sociology has been taught in Canada since the beginning of the century, it is by no means as developed a discipline as it is, for instance, in the United States. This lag prevails not only because of societal influences in general, but also because research funds for the social sciences have been shockingly scarce and continue to be so to a great extent.[3] Therefore, Canadian sociologists frequently do not have the opportunity to engage in long-term research projects that would advance the field, for they do not have access to funds or to research assistants. It is consequently not too surprising if, as Timlin and Faucher correctly point out, sociology in Canada has not aroused international attention, nor (can we add?) national interest.[4]

Related to these points is the fact that as of 1973 we in Canada have not developed an original sociology, that is, one with a distinct orientation. As many observers have pointed out, Quebec, at the confluence of the French and American traditions and with a specific view on the global society, is perhaps closest to having achieved such distinctiveness.[5] It is possible that, in view of our geographic, economic, and cultural proxim-

2. Desmond M. Connor and James E. Curtis, *Sociology and Anthropology in Canada*, Montreal: Canadian Sociology and Anthropology Association, September, 1970.
3. For data on social science research funding in Canada, see Fred Schindeler and C. Michael Lanphier, "Social Science Research and Participatory Democracy in Canada," reprinted in *Social and Cultural Change in Canada*, edited by W.E. Mann, Toronto: Copp Clark, vol. 2, 1970, pp. 64-87.
4. Mabel E. Timlin and Albert Faucher, *The Social Sciences in Canada: Two Studies*, Ottawa: Social Science Research Council of Canada, 1968, pp. 37-38.
5. Frank G. Vallee and Donald R. Whyte, "Canadian Society: Trends and Perspectives," in *Canadian Society: Sociological Perspectives*, abridged edition,

ity to the United States, there is no necessity or even possibility for Canadian sociology to branch out in a unique direction.[6] Such a distinct perspective may be difficult to achieve for a long time to come for still another reason: as of 1967, 72% of the sociologists practicing in Canada had received their graduate training in the United States. This factor certainly contributes to the merging of the two anglophone sociologies and to the hiatus between the two Canadian sociologies.[7]

Another related obstacle is less frequently mentioned by sociologists. We are referring to a process of self-selection among English-speaking sociologists in years past whereby those who were the most likely to make major contributions to the field have chosen to remain in the United States because the American academic structure has been more conducive to research and to the rewarding of prominent intellectuals.[8] In other words, our structure and our institutions were not sufficiently competitive, and top sociologists who later established themselves in Canada very likely did so at a personal cost.

Another aspect of the dilemma is that very few well-known

---

edited by Bernard R. Blishen et al., Toronto: Macmillan, 1968, pp. 556-575; and Philippe Garique, "French Canada: A Case Study in Sociological Analysis," Canadian Review of Sociology and Anthropology, 1, 1964, pp. 186-193. See also Jean-Charles Falardeau, L'essor des sciences sociales au Canada français, Quebec: Ministère des affaires culturelles, 1964, especially p. 58, and G. Fortin, "Le Quebec: Une société globale à la recherche d'elle-même," Recherches sociographiques, 8, 1967, pp. 7-13. As a further indicator of the differences between Quebec sociology and Canadian sociology, we note that Guy Rocher's translated textbook, A General Introduction to Sociology: A Theoretical Perspective (Toronto: Macmillan, 1972), does not discuss social problems. Rossides does, however. (David W. Rossides, Society as a Functional Process: An Introduction to Sociology, Toronto: McGraw-Hill of Canada, 1968.)

6. Rossides, ibid., p. vi.

7. Least one attribute this phenomenon strictly to the Americans, it must be noted that all of Canada produced only eleven doctorates in sociology over the five year period from 1965 to 1970, and, by the count in Connor and Curtis (op. cit.), twenty-two from 1924 to 1967. For differences between francophone and anglophone sociologists, see John Harp and James E. Curtis, "Linguistic Communication and Sociology: Data from the Canadian Case," in Social Process and Institution: The Canadian Case, by James E. Gallagher and Ronald D. Lambert, Toronto: Holt, Rinehart and Winston of Canada, 1971, pp. 57-71.

8. This observation also applies to other social sciences. See Timlin and Faucher, op. cit., p. 55.

sociology journals are published in Canada. In fact, none carries as much international prestige as the several major American journals so easily accessible to Canadians. And the few Canadian journals which exist tend, at times, to encourage publication of research on certain specific topics, thus further reducing the likelihood that sociologists with other interests will publish in Canada. This process is further exacerbated by another result of the American graduate training received by the majority of sociologists in this country. The reference group of Canadian scholars is American—perhaps to a considerable extent unavoidably so. And, while a great percentage of Canadian sociologists belong to the American Sociological Association, and therefore subscribe to its journals and attend its meetings, the reverse does not occur. It often happens, therefore, that when Canadian-based sociologists initiate a research project, they intend to have their results published in the United States. In other words, it can be said that the reference group of most Canadian sociologists is in great part American, and that this state of affairs is reinforced and probably made unavoidable by the paucity of publication outlets of international stature in Canada.

What the points raised above mean is that much sociological writing must be intended for an American publisher, if it is to be disseminated at all. It also means that, in order for their research results to be accepted by American journals, Canadian sociologists have to deemphasize national content, although this constraint is presently easing. We therefore hope that this series will contribute to an increasing sense of self-awareness among Canadian-based sociologists. We are confident that it will contribute to the synthesizing of data that have already been gathered in Canada, and that it will point out gaps and encourage researchers to focus their attention on areas of deficiency both theoretically and empirically. By the same token, authors in the series may indirectly invite more generous government support of research in the social sciences.

Richard L. Henshel
Anne-Marie Henshel

FEBRUARY, 1973

Introduction

The focus of this book is on the definitional aspects of social problems rather than on their alleviation or resolution.[1] The latter, along with questions of measurement and evaluation, is the topic of *Reacting to Social Problems*—in many respects the companion to this book.[2] The orientation of the book is not confined strictly to problem-centred theories; our approach is relatively broad and we have frequently employed an historical framework as well as a sociology of knowledge perspective. Although we cannot fully subscribe to the implications of Blumer's thesis, we have taken as our point of departure his statement that "social problems are fundamentally products of a process of *collective definition* instead of existing independently as a set of objective social arrangements with an intrinsic make up."[3] It has become increasingly clear, since the First Edition of this book was published in 1973, that the definitional processes are crucial.[4]

A second theme running through this book is that world view and ideology are the chief determinants of societal reaction to social problems, and that this is the case whether it is the world view of the local law enforcement official that is being analyzed or that of the sociologist. It follows that a study is needed which

1. See Amitai Etzioni, "Toward a Theory of Societal Guidance," *American Journal of Sociology*, 73, 1967, pp. 173-187.
2. Richard L. Henshel, *Reacting to Social Problems*, Toronto: Academic Press Canada, 1976.
3. Herbert Blumer, "Social Problems as Collective Behavior," *Social Problems*, 18, 1971, p.298, italics ours.
4. See *The Collective Definition of Deviance*, edited by F. James Davis and Richard Stivers, New York: Free Press, 1975.

treats both the stereotypes of the policeman on the beat and the sociologist in the classroom in a common frame of reference, or at least considers their positions as perceptual matters which deserve similar treatment. Such is the point of view of this book. What happens before and after x breaks into the neighbourhood bank is a result of the world views of legislators (perhaps long dead), intellectuals, experts on neighbourhood bank robberies, the police officers who capture x, the newspeople who report it, and x's own viewpoint. This is not to say that we will treat all perspectives with equal sympathy, but we will treat them all as perspectives.

Central to our personal views and therefore recurrent in the text are questions of objectivity and of values. While we present as many viewpoints as possible on any topic covered, we also raise questions, many of which have no clear-cut answers. And each answer begets more questions. Social problems do not lend themselves to study as unambiguously as mechanical or biological situations. The very nature of the problems (that is, their social and human aspects, combined with the social and human nature of the student) renders the entire process very difficult, and entanglements with perceptions, values, and ideologies are unavoidable. It is one purpose of sociology as a discipline to provide a framework within which such extra-scientific factors will be recognized, analyzed, and placed into perspective.

Readers will notice that we have concentrated our discussion on a limited number of social problems, such as crime and mental illness. This is an open reflection of the degree of interest we as individual sociologists have in the various topics that constitute social problems. It would be surprising if anyone were equally interested or equally versed in all problem areas. When necessary, we have drawn upon examples from the appropriate subjects, but a work which outlines perspectives on social problems need not touch on every topical area in order to highlight the key issues. The reader should also not expect "Canadian content" to be the specific focus of this book, for we are herein dealing with theoretical and conceptual questions that transcend national boundaries. Although we have preferred Canadian sources and Canadian examples when available, the reader is referred to the topical monographs in this series for specifically Canadian material.[5]

This monograph is designed both for students having only a brief acquaintance with the field of sociology and, as a means of integrating otherwise scattered material, for professional sociologists. Certain sections are specifically directed to students, whereas others address themselves to a mixed audience. Since certain presentations relate to discussions that are met only through a more advanced familiarization with sociology, we have sought to simplify matters for the beginning student by offering a bibliographical *glossary* at the end of the book. This glossary serves two purposes. First, it offers one or two definitions of certain concepts met in the body of the text. To this end we have sought those definitions on which many sociologists seem to agree by taking those that are recurrent in the literature. And to give a wider sense of the literature, we have tried as much as possible to quote definitions from prominent texts rather than supplying new versions. Second, the glossary frequently offers the student references to one or two well-known, comprehensive works related to the concept or theory under consideration, thereby providing additional basic citations when further research or inquiry is desired. An *asterisk* in the text indicates the first mention of a word appearing in the glossary.

In the First Edition in 1973 we organized the material to promote the development of our themes of collective definition and reaction to social problems. It is encouraging to note that several prominent discussions of the definitional aspect of social problems that have since appeared have generated much the same categories of definers as our own.[6] Because of the success of the First Edition, we have decided to leave the book's organization essentially unchanged, although, as indicated in the Preface, the contents have been revised and expanded. The

5. See the front-matter of this book for a list of the titles and authors in the Canadian Social Problems Series.
6. Richard Hawkins and Gary Tiedeman, *The Creation of Deviance*, Columbus, Ohio: Charles Merrill, 1975, especially pp. 82-86; Armand L. Mauss, *Social Problems as Social Movements*, Philadelphia: Lippincott, 1975; Malcolm Spector and John Kitsuse, *Constructing Social Problems*, Menlo Park, Cal.: Cummings, 1977.

first two chapters introduce the controversial nature of the social problems concept, first from a definitional review of social problems in general and then from a historical perspective. Chapter 2 also reviews the historical development of two case studies problems, mental illness and poverty. Chapter 3 discusses five major approaches to social problems in their chronological order of prominence—pathology, disorganization, conflict, deviance, and labeling. In Chapters 4 through 6 the definitional "act" in the emergence of social problems is further explored, with a focus on the various agents who may be involved. Chapter 4 first explores the general effect of life experiences on outlook and world view, then examines the roles of the victim and of the communications mass media. Chapter 5 discusses moral entrepreneurship, including a look at both religiously-based fundamentalism and egalitarian movements. Chapter 6 looks at the roles of the intellectual, the social problems expert, and the psychiatric community. In Chapter 7, the selection of individuals for involuntary "treatment" is explored in relation to the stereotypes and ideologies of the labelers.

1 What Is a Social Problem?

> *I cannot refute the learned arguments for the relativity of ethical values, but I refuse to believe that the only thing wrong about wanton cruelty is that I don't like it.*
> —Bertrand Russell

One of the main themes running through this book is the existence of a wide divergence of opinion concerning most aspects of social problems. Subject to disagreement are such questions as: Which situations constitute social problems? Who should decide what a social problem is? How should social problems be treated? Who should pay for the treatment and who should dispense it? Dissensus on these and related questions cannot merely be attributed to confused terminology or ignorance; it reflects ideological differences in the population at large, as well as among social scientists. Answers to these questions reflect one's view of the world and how it should be changed. Although reasonable agreement exists in theory about the definition of what a social problem is, we will see that matters become more involved when we confront theory with reality. This chapter is, therefore, more than a simple definitional exercise: it is an examination of the consequences of stressing one ideological aspect over another. To start with, we present a definition on which there is substantial agreement among sociologists, but from then on we will follow a path that will take us some distance from this comfortable state of consensus.

A social problem has been defined as "a condition affecting a significant number of people in ways considered undesirable, about which it is felt something can be done through collective social action."[1] The key word in this definition is "social" and, in an attempt to differentiate social problems from other categories of deleterious conditions, three criteria are often used: social problems can be defined as those which are social in origin, social in definition, and social in treatment.[2] But, depending on the sociologists' orientation, there are important variations in the relative significance accorded these points. How various conditions fit into sociological conceptions of what social problems are will be explored as we discuss the three criteria.

SOCIAL IN ORIGIN

Social problems will be defined in this monograph as situations related to social factors that adversely affect significant numbers of individuals in a similar way. Such a definition implies that the origins, or certain aspects thereof, have been *diagnosed* as social. Social problems are thereby differentiated from other conditions which affect large segments of the population in a way that is not perceived as being social. The emphasis with respect to the criterion of origins is on *perception*. For instance, poliomyelitis used to be a serious problem before the Salk vaccine. But its origin or cause is perceived to be purely biological. It is a physical disease which is, insofar as we know, unrelated to social factors. Does this mean that, even when it affected thousands of persons, it was not a social problem? From one perspective, it was a social problem because

---

1. Paul B. Horton and Gerald R. Leslie, *The Sociology of Social Problems*, fourth edition, New York: Appleton-Century-Crofts, 1970, p. 4. A definition written in 1923 illustrates the extent of agreement or borrowing across the decades: "A social problem is a problem which actually or potentially affects large numbers of people in a common way so that it may best be solved by some measure or measures applied to the problem as a whole rather than by dealing with each individual as an isolated case, or which requires concerted or organized human action." Quoted in James H.S. Bossard, *Social Change and Social Problems*, revised edition, New York: Harper and Brothers, 1938, p. 2.
2. Horton and Leslie, *ibid.*, p. 6.

of the very fact that it affected large numbers of individuals. People were, in addition, aware of the gravity of the situation and urgently wanted a solution; therefore, it was also social in definition (the second criterion). And Dentler maintains that it is the matter of collective social responsibility that gives a problem its social aspect, rather than its origin.[3] Merton adopts a similar perspective and prefers to abandon the distinction stressing origins.[4] Thus, such an undesirable condition as polio can be viewed as a social problem if we eliminate the criterion of social origins.

As it is obvious that with such a widening of the definition virtually every public problem could become a social problem, we have to narrow down the definition for the purpose of sociology.[5] To return to the example of polio, it is improbable that a sociologist could become involved in such a problem as a direct subject of study because, outside of the fact that it affects human beings and that it may be defined as a problem by society, it does not lie within the social realm in terms either of perceived origin or cure. For sociologists, polio is not an object of study because we view its origins in terms of biological causes. However, the social organization of medical research and treatment *is* a topic for sociology, as the social organization for research on any subject may be. And the attitude of the population vis-à-vis medical problems is also a topic of concern for sociologists, as is the quality of life of the individuals affected by any medical problem.

3. Robert A. Dentler, *Major Social Problems*, second edition, Chicago: Rand McNally, 1972, p. 6.
4. Robert K. Merton, "Social Problems and Sociological Theory," in *Contemporary Social Problems*, third edition, edited by Robert K. Merton and Robert Nisbet, New York: Harcourt Brace Jovanovich, 1971, p. 802. He also retains what we call "disasters" within the nomenclature of social problems, whereas we prefer to view social problems as phenomena that are lasting in their origins or causes, or that are recurrent. While a flood may have lasting consequences that will affect people psychologically and socially, it is, in terms of origins, a one-time "act of God." But were floodings recurrent in some areas, they could be included in our classification.
5. It should be noted that, in spite of the best definitions, the traditional demarcations of sociological interest in social problems are at least partly arbitrary. Thus economic cycles (depressions and inflationary periods) are properly social problems but are treated only by economists.

Cancer presents a related but different dilemma in terms of definition. It is a major human problem and is recognized as such by everyone. For sociologists, cancer is not intrinsically a social problem because of its biological nature. But cigarette smoking is causally related to lung cancer[6] and smoking is a cultural phenomenon (exacerbated by advertising, socialization, and peer groups); hence, cancer is a social problem by virtue of its relationship to a cultural act: smoking cigarettes.[7] The same remarks can be advanced with regard to the correlations between some forms of cancer and exposure to certain substances, such as asbestos, in the workplace. Workplace exposure is closely related to social class, and so too the incidence of some forms of cancer is closely linked to social class. It is therefore accurate to posit that, because of the social aspects of the origins of cancer, this problem is of some concern to sociologists.[8]

Pollution is another problem which is of interest here. Like lung cancer, pollution is a borderline case. Pollution is certainly a human problem because it adversely affects entire populations. In addition, it is social in definition because a segment of public opinion is aroused against it and wants the situation brought under control. But, from the perspective of origins, pollution is not social because it is produced by chemical components that are not social per se, just as polio was produced by a virus and was therefore biological. However, inasmuch as carbon monoxide, as an instance of pollution, is produced by machinery which is, in turn, produced by human beings, we have a cultural component in the origin of this problem. In addition, people have now become aware of the noxious consequences of the release of carbon monoxide in the air, and their refusal to cope with this problem, or with conflicts over the cost of its control, are definitely social phenomena. From that point of view, it can be said that pollution is indeed a social problem, even in origin.

6. See *Smoking and Health*, Report of the Advisory Committee to the Surgeon General, Washington: U.S. Government Printing Office, 1964.
7. The terms "social" and "cultural" are used interchangeably here for purposes of simplification.
8. See the discussion in Chapters 13 and 14 of *Smoking and Health, op. cit.*

In contrast to the above difficulty, consider the case of several hundred poor, black victims of syphilis in the American South who, in an organized experiment started in the 1930's, went for decades without treatment in order to furnish a medical baseline for what untreated syphilis does to the brain and other organs. The problem in such a case is discrimination based on race. Although race is a biological category, sociologists can certainly study and contribute to the redress of this and similar phenomena, and certainly such discrimination is a social problem. Likewise, although leprosy is obviously of biological origin, some experts regard it as more of a social problem than a tropical disease. The victims of leprosy are treated as pariahs by many societies, even though they pose virtually no health threat to others. Here, again, the problem is very largely social in nature.

In contrast to the examples of polio, cancer, pollution, and leprosy, which are difficult to classify if we faithfully insist on applying the criterion of social origin, there are those problems which spring directly from social forces and their interrelations and, especially, there are those on which there is consensus on the pre-eminence of the social origin (although not necessarily so on the causes themselves).

Let us consider the example of crimes against property. There is nothing in a criminal act of this type that is not social in nature. Under one interpretation, individuals are driven to property crimes by personal concerns which spring largely from the situation the person is in and the alternatives the society offers, or which the person perceives the society as offering. As many observers have noted, our society places a high emphasis on economic gain and material rewards. In addition, this society's values are such that individuals are expected to achieve in the material realm and, in principle, the system is supposed to provide individuals with institutionally acceptable means of reaching this goal. Equality of opportunity is the motto, although considerable evidence points to strong limitations on it. On the one hand, therefore, we have a cultural ethos emphasizing material achievement, frequently attainable only through formal education channels. On the other hand, the society is so structured that some cannot reach this goal even if highly qualified.[9] Legitimate opportunities are not always within reach, be it because of poverty, behavioural patterns learned through socialization, or other socio-cultural factors. Some individuals who cannot achieve through the regular channels or who want to climb more rapidly may turn to illegal means which are also provided by our society.[10]

In the above analysis, we have presented two factors that are typically considered socio-cultural: cultural goals and social structure. Other theories of crime causation also emphasize various social factors such as family influences, peer group associations, deviant role models, assimilation of deviant codes of conduct, cultural conflict, awareness of legal loopholes, and so on.[11] On the whole, the criterion of social origin is useful in delineating the area of social problems for the purpose of *sociological* analysis; however, the various social ramifications of certain human problems (such as cancer) diminish the definitional suitability of this criterion.

SOCIAL IN DEFINITION

According to Tallman and McGee, "a social problem exists if a sizable group of individuals share the view that a given event

9. Several studies have indicated that, for instance, parental socio-economic status is an important factor in the probability that a person will be able to pursue higher education. In Canada, see: P.M. George and H.Y. Kim, "Social Factors and Educational Aspirations of Canadian High School Students," in *Social Process and Institution: The Canadian Case*, by James E. Gallagher and Ronald D. Lambert, Toronto: Holt, Rinehart and Winston, 1971, pp. 352-363. In the United States, see: Natalie Rogoff Ramsoy, "On the Flow of Talent in Society," *Acta Sociologica*, 9, 1965, pp. 152-174.

10. Students of deviance will recognize that this discussion is directly borrowed from Robert K. Merton, *Social Theory and Social Structure*, revised and enlarged edition, Glencoe, Ill.: Free Press, 1957, pp. 132 ff. See also Robin M. Williams, Jr., "Relative Deprivation," in *The Idea of Social Structure*, edited by Lewis A. Coser, New York: Harcourt Brace Jovanovich, 1975, especially p. 355.

11. This view of criminality disregards biological theories of crime such as chromosomal abnormalities. However, even if such tentative theories are established as operant among certain criminals, they would account for only a small part of total crime, and even then cultural and social factors are apparently involved in virtually all cases.

or process is problematic."[12] The implication is that a situation is a problem *only when so perceived.* Kavolis, among others, refers to this as the "public awareness conception" of social problems.[13] Blum adopts a similar perspective and points out that "it is not the event but the way the event is treated that defines the problem."[14] And Blumer has made this emphasis on *subjective* (as opposed to *objective* or de facto) factors the central thesis of an article: "Social problems are fundamentally products of a process of collective definition instead of existing independently as a set of objective social arrangements."[15]

This is a provocative and controversial statement, for if we define a social problem as existing only when a condition is *perceived* as undesirable, it means that a social problem is first and above all the theoretical construct of certain people.[16] From the objective perspective on the other hand, a social problem exists as soon as a significant number of individuals are adversely affected by a phenomenon related to social factors, even if no one recognizes it. But Horton and Leslie state that "no condition, no matter how dramatic or shocking to someone else, is a social problem unless and until the values of a considerable number of people within the society define it as a problem."[17] This point of view requires further attention as it pertains to the critical questions of who the definers of a social problem are and how a situation becomes labeled as a problem—topics that will be the focus of Chapters 4 through 6. Horton and Leslie go

12. Irving Tallman and Reese McGee, "Definition of a Social Problem," in *Handbook on the Study of Social Problems*, edited by Erwin O. Smigel, Chicago: Rand McNally, 1971, p. 40.

13. Vytautas Kavolis, *Comparative Perspectives on Social Problems*, Boston: Little, Brown and Co., 1969.

14. Alan F. Blum, "Methods for Recognizing, Formulating, and Describing Social Problems," in *Handbook on the Study of Social Problems*, edited by Erwin O. Smigel, Chicago: Rand McNally, 1971, p. 180.

15. Herbert Blumer, "Social Problems as Collective Behavior," *Social Problems*, 18, 1971, p. 298. See also Leonard Reissman, "The Solution Cycle of Social Problems," *American Sociologist*, 7, February, 1972, pp. 7-9.

16. Sociologists such as Coser, Dentler, and Merton have recognized and discussed this situation. See Lewis A. Coser, "Sociology of Poverty," *Social Problems*, 13, 1965, pp. 140-148; Dentler, *op. cit.*; Merton, 1971, *op. cit.*

17. Horton and Leslie, *op. cit.*, p. 5 (italics in the original text eliminated).

further and add that "when a condition affects enough people so that many of them take notice and begin to talk and write about it, a social problem exists. . . . When numerous articles appear, it is clear that the condition has attracted widespread concern and has become a social problem."[18]

In other words, these writers say, a condition is a social problem only if it is noticed, or if concern arises, especially, as implied in the Tallman and McGee quote—and here is the additional element—by people who control societal resources, in this case the mass media. While such a definition appears biased from the point of view of the sufferers, it may, nevertheless, correspond to reality in terms of the treatment or solution of a problem.

Let us examine this apparent ambiguity. On the one hand, we reject this restrictive definition as unrepresentative of reality but agree that it reflects, in practical terms, the way social problems do or do not get treated. First, objectively speaking, we maintain that a social problem exists as soon as significant numbers of people are adversely affected by some condition. For instance, if many Indians are indigently poor, suffer from ill health, are chronically unemployed, *and* feel their deprivation, this is a social problem whether others notice it or not. It need not wait for our goodwill, nor for changes in our value orientations. The situation may not have been conceptualized as a problem for many decades—perhaps because we believed in the supremacy of Western civilization, or because Indians and Inuit are geographically too distant to concern our daily lives.[19] But during all those silent decades, the problem was nevertheless real. More recently, we have become enlightened enough to make the diagnosis. Our new attitude merely reinforces the existence of the problem in terms of social visibility and attention, but does not create it. Merton invokes a helpful

18. *Ibid.*, p. 4. Surveys of what people think the major social problems are thus become significant. See in the Canadian context Reginald W. Bibby, "Consensus in Diversity: An Examination of Canadian Problem Perception," *International Journal of Comparative Sociology*, 20, 1979, pp. 274-282.
19. For a similar opinion on the effect of social (and physical) distance, see Merton, 1971, *op. cit.*, p. 812.

terminological distinction here by speaking of *manifest* social problems—those which are recognized—and *latent* social problems—those which are real but unnoticed.[20]

This discussion brings us to a consideration of whether those who suffer from a condition should be the only ones to decide on the definitional nature of their situation. This is a very difficult question to settle. In Chapters 4 and 7, for instance, we will ask with respect to emotional problems whether anything should be done to help the individuals afflicted if they do not perceive their situation as harmful. The same question could be asked of the Inuit or any other geographically marginal minority group. If *they* do not perceive their situation as problematic, is it? In other words, by our standards, they could be poor, unemployed, in ill health, and chronically subject to alcoholism. Yet, if they do not see anything abnormal in their plight nor feel deprived, do we have the right (or perhaps the obligation) to diagnose their situation as a social problem and, consequently, initiate programmes to improve it?[21]

Minority groups such as the Inuit have a culture of their own, with a distinct set of values. Saying that by all (our) objective standards they are poor and that poverty in general is a problem may mean denying the validity of non-material values such as asceticism that we do not share with them. Negating these values places us in the elitist position of saying that we know what is good for a people even though they may not want it. This was a problem common to most justifications of imperialism in the nineteenth century: it was supposedly the "white man's burden" to lead inferior peoples into the "light of civilization," but how could the presumed superiority of European values be a certainty? In point of fact it was superior military technology that established and perpetuated the colon-

20. Merton, 1971, *ibid.*, pp. 806-810.
21. This question is important from yet another perspective. Remedial programmes frequently carry the germs of unanticipated harms (unanticipated consequences) which only magnify the problem they were originally set to alleviate. Intervention can therefore worsen a situation. For an extended discussion of this difficulty see Merton, 1957, *op. cit.* and Richard L. Henshel, *Reacting to Social Problems*, Toronto: Academic Press Canada, 1976, Chapter 3.

ial system.[22] Cultural relativism* recognizes the validity and equality of all cultures and, therefore, the right to cultural self-determination.

The principle of non-interference in the affairs of other cultural groups (at times called isolationism in world politics) is not in itself an absolute answer, however: it leaves the door open to frightening moral dilemmas. What of the Jewish holocaust before and during World War II? Following a policy of non-interference, France and Great Britain abstained from intervention in the German situation during the greater part of the 1930's. This abstention—motivated by political rather than value reasons—ultimately cost millions of lives, and caused unprecedented suffering. The Nazi holocaust led Herskovitz, a prominent adherent of cultural relativism, into the depths of an ethical as well as a philosophical dilemma. We are comforted by the thought that the Nazi era was an exceptional period; perhaps the principle of non-interference is intact. Yet, there is no certainty that similar events will not be repeated. For instance, mass slaughters periodically take place between certain African nation-tribes. Therefore, we are still left with the dilemma since "exceptions" to ethical and cultural relativism, such as genocide of entire populations, recur again and again. The resolution of such ethical questions has proven elusive.[23]

With regard to the Inuit, the Indians, or similar geographically cohesive groups, the political concept of pluralism allows, at least in principle, for cultural (if not economic) autonomy. But, in those situations where this pluralism cannot apply in its totality because the minority groups are too closely interwoven with the rest of society, what is to be done? Closely related to this question is the dilemma posed by the case of emotionally disturbed individuals. The latter are situated within the major-

22. The only difference between the present-day situation and that of nineteenth century colonizers and missionaries is the particular elitist values of the dominant group.
23. Bell and Mau suggest that the possibility of common and universal values should be investigated. See Wendell Bell and James A. Mau, "Images of the Future: Theory and Research Strategies," in *The Sociology of the Future*, edited by Wendell Bell and James A. Mau, New York: Russell Sage, 1971, p. 38.

ity culture, and this is, therefore, no longer a question of cultural relativism or pluralism but one of intra-cultural deviance. The psychological state of certain individuals may be viewed, from the vantage point of the rest of society, as harmful to those afflicted, and even to the society as a whole. Since this is not a question of imposing one's standard on another cultural group, interference (psychiatric treatment) could be said to be more appropriate within this context than in the cross-cultural example. But here other complications arise because of the difficulty of diagnosis and the potential for serious abuse in the labeling and treatment processes. We will discuss this question in Chapter 7.

Let us briefly return to the complexity of our decision regarding the subjective definition of social problems. We rejected the subjective conception as deficient for purposes of determining what is problematic, but, at the same time, saw it as representative of reality in terms of whether or not remedial action occurs. The act of defining a phenomenon as a social problem implies that the situation is undesirable *and* that someting should be done to remedy it. Or, as the definition quoted at the outset of the chapter said, it implies that "collective action" is necessary—even if by collective we only mean the action of a society's leaders. A latent social problem may exist for decades but never be diagnosed as such; therefore, society will not be moved to act collectively to solve it. Consequently, a situation is defined as problematic so as to hopefully benefit from the application of this adjective. Before a label was bestowed it was a problem but there was little hope that any relief would be forthcoming. There is, consequently, considerable utility for the subjective or public-awareness conception of social problems in terms of estimating the likelihood of treatment.

A condition becomes defined as problematic when a substantial number of people, be they sufferers or observers, notice the situation, define it as undesirable and, therefore, as in need of public action. But in one sense the situation will become an officially recognized social problem only when people who are *strategically located* in society's power structure deign to acknowledge its existence. Others might have spoken about it previously but with so little social influence that not even their peers would accept their definition. As soon as a relatively important segment of the population makes the diagnosis, a "new" social problem is seen. The segment may be important numerically and have access to the political power structure. In such a case, it may exert pressure on those in power.[24] Or, a segment may be important not because of its size but because of its strategic location. We could include in this category members of the government, the intelligentsia,* the press, executives, organized labour, students, and even some minority groups who are the victims of social problems. A social problem in terms of public attention is one that has become read about, seen and heard on television, discussed at cocktail parties, and lectured about in classrooms.

There are certain social conditions that facilitate the transformation of an objective deleterious situation into a manifest social problem. For instance, we quoted Tallman and McGee to the effect that a social problem exists if "a sizable group of individuals shares the view that a given event or process is problematic."[25] By this definition, certain phenomena will more readily become accepted as social problems, because of numbers and because of public exposure through the media. Sociological investigations of the process of social influence allow us to enumerate some of the major facilitating factors involved: the number of people believed to be affected; the perceived gravity of their affliction; the perceived injustice of their condition; whether those who cause their misfortune do so deliberately; the type of group which first diagnoses the inequity; the type of group disseminating knowledge on the problem; the means the group adopts to publicize the situation; the degree of access to the public of these groups; their degree of access to those in positions of power; the ideological and cultural readiness of the society; the strength of the groups whose vested interest would

24. But a segment of the population can be very numerous and yet be excluded from the political system. The situation of the black population in the Republic of South Africa is a case in point.
25. Tallman and McGee, *op. cit.*, p. 40.

be hurt by a redress of the situation; and the potential degree of harm to such groups.

Because so many factors are involved before a condition is publicly defined as problematic, the restriction of "social problem" to a condition perceived by a public appears to do violence to the term's conventional meaning. Tallman and McGee, among others, relate the urgency of a problem to its "magnitude," and add that magnitude can be substantiated by noting (a) the number of people affected and (b) the intensity of feeling the problem generates.[26] We feel that the first factor, along with intensity of suffering, is perhaps the only reliable indicator in determining whether a social problem exists; passion or feelings against a situation by groups attempting to solve it is a less objective criterion, and a more volatile one. It is volatile because the intensity of people's feelings is subject to manipulation for various reasons and from various quarters. A group having easy access to the media or to official communication channels can educate the public in such a way as to bring about passionate feelings and ill-founded responses. To the Nazis, for instance, the existence of Jews in the Fatherland was a social problem, and they systematically set about heightening anti-semitic feelings through the mass media. The long-run bureaucratization of the "final solution" the Jewish question, and its resemblance to an attack on a traditional social problem, should serve as an object lesson in the unreliability of passion as a convincing criterion of the worthiness of a movement against "problems."[27] The criterion of passion cannot be used in a definition of a social problem, even though it may be essential in terms of coming to grips with treatment.

26. *Ibid.*, p. 42.
27. See Raul Hilbert, "The Destruction of the European Jews," in *Mass Society in Crisis*, edited by Bernard Rosenberg *et al.*, New York: Macmillan, 1964. Probably the most pronounced advocacy of the subjective definition of social problems is contained in Malcolm Spector and John Kitsuse, *Constructing Social Problems*, Menlo Park, Cal.: Benjamin/Cummings, 1977. Readers desiring a further examination of this viewpoint should consult this excellent treatment.

SOCIAL IN TREATMENT

Clearly, a condition need not be erased or effectively treated to be a real social problem. Indeed, it could be stated that many social problems, even some that are socially recognized, are never treated. Perhaps powerful groups or persons block the treatment for personal reasons. Perhaps resolving one social problem would create others.[28] Perhaps its resolution would do away with other highly valued aspects of a society.[29] Perhaps the causes are unknown and the society must depend on the tedious process of trial and error in order to remedy a situation. We can therefore conclude by saying that a social problem has to have at least the *potential* to be socially remedied.

If the origins of a problem are perceived to be social, the remedy will also be social in most cases. If we once more return to the example of polio, the treatment will be related to its biological causes and, even though money and social activities are required to apply it, the remedy will consist largely of vaccination and hospitalization for those already afflicted. Unless discrimination against a group or social class exists in terms of treatment, treatment will be of no concern to the student of social problems.[30] Therefore, polio does not fulfill the third defining criterion of a social problem: it is not social in treatment, not even potentially so. (We have also seen that it is not social in origin.) However, if we deal with an example such as that of pollution, although the treatment measures will be largely physical (design of different power sources, building of new treatment plants), there will also be such measures involved as convincing the public of the gravity of the problem, and educating people to accept the required life style changes,

28. Some economists, for example, have maintained that a "trade-off" between unemployment and inflation exists: according to this perspective, as one of these problems is reduced below a certain level it automatically brings about an increase in the other. We do not wish to take sides in this question, but *if* the theory is correct we have an unsolvable set of social problems. See an extensive discussion of such "trade-offs" in Henshel, *op. cit.*, pp. 52-54.

29. See, for instance, the suggested causes of crime in Daniel Bell, "Crime as an American Way of Life," *Antioch Review*, 13, 1953, pp. 131-154.

30. Medical sociologists will study various aspects of medical treatment (patient-doctor relationships, hospital and ward structure) but will do so outside of the social problem framework, unless discrimination exists.

as well as re-directing the lives of so many whose livelihoods depend on activities that entail pollution and the depletion of the environment.[31] Factors such as social power and the pursuit of profit minimize the effectiveness of educational efforts. So, with pollution, although its immediate cause is physico-chemical, and although its ultimate treatment will also be physical and material, the decisional aspects take on unusual importance, making this a marginally social type of problem.

Another example discussed in the section on origins was that of crimes against property. In order to alleviate this problem, we will probably have to turn to solutions which are social in nature.[32] Assuming that we have some understanding of the genesis of crime, and that our diagnosis points to cultural goals, what remedy could be prescribed? As one example, the society could de-emphasize material rewards and offer new goals to its members—although these new goals may themselves become a springboard for other types of problems later on. Or, in terms of the structure of the society, true equality of opportunity in all spheres might be reached, whereas we now have only theoretical equality.[33] Other approaches might also be attempted, depending on our assumptions about the causes of crime.[34] Some of these approaches might be so costly, in their effect on other, desirable features of the culture or social structure, that the cure becomes worse than the disease.[35] But in virtually all approaches, the dominant features of treatment would be sociocultural; property crime is clearly a social problem.

31. See Kimon Valaskakis *et al.*, *The Conserver Society*, Don Mills, Ont.: Fitzhenry and Whiteside, 1979.
32. For a different view see Amitai Etzioni and Richard Remp, *Technological Shortcuts in the Treatment of Social Problems*, New York: Russell Sage, 1972.
33. But this might bring about new problems because of a "drainage of talent" from the lower class. See Michael Young's hypothetical description in *The Rise of the Meritocracy*, New York: Random House, 1959. Etzioni has suggested that in studying causes we should virtually ignore those we can do nothing about, and focus on the "strategic" causes which, if research should so indicate, we could actually treat.
34. One need not have knowledge of all, or even most, of the factors behind a social problem to begin work on its removal. If the demand for a "war against double parkers" was sufficiently strong, double parking could be eliminated by mandatory $1,000 fines and two policemen on every block—even with minimal knowledge of why people double park.
35. For instance, it could be objected that the "solution" proposed in the footnote above would be exceedingly irrational behaviour, and indeed one aim

CONCLUSION

The question we have raised is: what constitutes a social problem? What criteria can we legitimately use to determine that one harmful condition affecting large numbers of individuals is a social problem whereas another harmful condition is not? Three commonly used criteria were discussed: social problems, it is said, are those conditions which are social in origin, in definition, and in treatment.

However, we saw that when we try to apply these criteria to specific examples of deleterious conditions, matters become more difficult. It is true that most of our social problems as currently defined in our society do fulfil these definitional requisites. Thus, conditions such as unemployment, poverty, crime, drug abuse and addiction, alcoholism, and mental illness are social in origin (until proven otherwise), in definition (we do recognize these conditions to be problems), and in treatment (various social programmes are initiated to alleviate them). But, when we turn to such conditions as cancer, we hesitate. It is of biological origin, we say, and therefore so is the treatment. But what of the socio-cultural component to cigarette smoking? In addition, even problems which are purely physical or biological in their origin have social dimensions if people are stigmatized by them, or receive differential levels of attention, treatment, or aid for them. And in cases such as pollution there is a social component to the mobilization of society to combat the problem.

But the issue which lies at the heart of the matter is whether social problems have an independent, objective reality apart from whether people view them as problematic. Blumer and others maintain that what is problematic is purely a matter of perspective—that members of society can collectively define virtually anything as a problem, and, equally, choose to ignore virtually anything. If the members of a society like something, can we define it as a social problem? Obviously not, and the

---

of the study of social problems is not only to determine what would "work" but what would be effective *at least cost* to what we hold dear.

Blumer perspective also fits well with modern notions in anthropology and theories of cultural and ethical relativity.

But there is a certain weakness to this point of view. It ignores or minimizes the fact that typically not all members of a culture agree on whether something is problematic.[36] Cultural relativity, or the relativistic perspective on social problems, places one in a "hands-off" dilemma: if no standards are sound, then we have nothing to say about objective criteria, and in effect the more influential of the social advocates succeeds in establishing its definition. (They might do so at any rate, but the relativistic position abdicates any responsibility of the sociologist.) Thus if Nazis define the existence of Jews as a social problem, they have a perfect right to do so, and to proceed to exterminate them. Of course the Jews also have a perfect right to disagree with this definition, but if the Nazis are stronger (and more numerous) than the Jews, and enforce their definition of the situation, who can say they are wrong? All values are relative, and there are no objective criteria for social problems.

The advocates of the public-awareness conception of social problems are among the most humanitarian of scholars; they would be the first to disagree with such a perversion. But such is the logical implication of their argument, in spite of its initial appeal and humanitarianism with respect to letting weak cultures define their own problems. On the other hand, if there *are* objective criteria for defining and determining social problems, what are they? We do not know, except by intuitive feelings, which are admittedly inadequate. Bertrand Russell captures the dilemma nicely in the humane lament in the epigraph at the beginning of this chapter.

Numerous efforts to resolve this problem have been forthcoming, all revolving around some form of "psychological ethics"—the attempt to ground ethical principles in studies of

36. Another difficulty that deserves brief mention is that, even when sociologists subscribe to the collective definition approach in theory, they do not always follow this rule in practice. Lauer surveyed textbooks on social problems and found a considerable disparity between the problems they treated and the concerns of the public as evidenced by some forty years of Gallup polls. See Robert H. Lauer, "Defining Social Problems: Public and Professional Perspectives," *Social Problems*, 22, October, 1976, pp. 122-134.

human psychology (or sociology). We will mention a few of the most insightful. Kavolis has attempted to delimit a common set of social problems by a comparative study of different cultures, locating "universals" that are defined as problems every- where.[37] Barrington Moore has maintained that, although hap- piness is achieved in exceedingly diverse ways, which are fluid and subjective, there is a substantial degree of unity or commonality in the ways people define misery or suffering. His suggestion is that we can move beyond cultural relativism in some cases by concentrating on conditions of extreme misery, on which there *is* substantial agreement.[38] Horowitz suggests that a transformation from "is" to "ought" can be made by defining a social problem in terms of the *disparity* between the existing situation and people's norms or values (for instance, equality of opportunity). In this case, both the situation and the values are matters of observable fact.[39] These and other con- tributions can make valuable inroads on the difficulty, but none are entirely successful in resolving it.

The focus of this book is on the subject raised in this chapter: the definitional aspect of social problems. Although we sub- scribe personally, in an intuitive way, to the idea of objectively existing problems, it is true that we can give no universal grounds for their detection. Certainly the question of social or collective definition—how, why, and when a society selects some social problems for attention and action—is critical. Public awareness is ordinarily essential for treatment to be initiated, except for rare cases of what might be called the natural remission of the problem. Seemingly paradoxically then, since we feel we must reject the extreme implications of

37. Kavolis, *op. cit* As Kavolis notes, universally held norms are very few and far between; practically speaking, the difficulties of such an approach are monumental. See also Graeme Newman, *Comparative Deviance: Perception and Law in Six Cultures*, New York: Elsevier, 1976.
38. Barrington Moore, Jr., *Reflections on the Causes of Human Misery*, Boston: Beacon, 1970. See his chapter, "On the Unity of Misery and the Diversity of Happiness."
39. Irving Louis Horowitz, *Professing Sociology*, Chicago: Aldine, 1968, pp. 80-100. One problem with such an approach is that it would not exclude Nazis

the perceptual or public awareness conception of social problems, the book has been oriented around the processes by which society actually derives its perceptions of social problems.

---

defining the presence of Jews in otherwise "clean" German cities as a social problem. (See earlier discussion.) For an overview of attempts to create a science of ethics that would give us absolute standards for social problems, see Chapter 5 of Robert Friedrichs, *A Sociology of Sociology*, New York: Free Press, 1970.

2 Emergence of the Social Problems Concept

> *Everything of importance has been said once before by someone who didn't discover it.*
>
> —Alfred North Whitehead

The social problems concept, as currently conceived, is a relatively recent development in the history of Western societies. Such conditions as mental disorder, crime, and poverty have always existed and are well documented in historical records. The deleterious quality of such conditions has been recognized in some manner in all known cultures. But these undesirable conditions were generally perceived within a fatalistic, religious, or military perspective. They were not generally seen as problems of well-being or of welfare that could be treated socially. Social problems in the past were defined as problems against order, against nature, against God, or, perhaps, as God's will. And it was only toward the end of the eighteenth century that many of the problems we now consider as social emerged as such in the public consciousness. This change toward a perception of problems was related to other developments in modern Western thought and social structure which will be discussed later in the chapter. First it is instructive to briefly examine how certain undesirable conditions were perceived and treated in earlier centuries. By way of illustration we will retrace historically the ideologies and approaches people have adopted toward mental disorders and poverty.

CASE I: MENTAL DISORDER

Because of religious beliefs and related ideological concepts of human nature, deviances in general were frequently perceived as punishment for sins (the Fall), as just manifestations of divine wrath, or even as indications of the subhumanity of those so affected. Treatment of the mentally ill was an obvious instance of this philosophy. Records from the later Middle Ages indicate that the agitated insane were kept confined in special "hospitals,"[1] usually in chains, thus underlining their commonality with the animal realm.[2] The emphasis was on protecting society against these "monsters" and on providing a means of social control within the confines of the religious doctrine of the day. "The scandal of madness showed men how close to animality their Fall could bring them; and at the same time how far divine mercy could extend when it consented to save man."[3] And, in many countries for which such information exists, we find that madmen—to use the language of the time—were exhibited to the public on certain days, especially Sundays, as a form of distraction, curiosity, and, especially, as a moral lesson.[4] It is said that for England the admission price for these spectacles was a penny, and "the annual revenue ... amounted to 400 pounds; which suggests the astonishingly high number of 96,000 visits per year."[5] It has been speculated that madmen replaced lepers as scapegoats in the public consciousness, and their forced isolation and the fears they evoked served to reinforce this state of affairs.[6] In addition, the insane were

1. The term "hospitals" was already old. In 1526, Vives defined them as places where the sick are cared for and fed, "where a certain number of paupers is supported, where boys and girls are reared ... where the insane are confined." This quote is from *Regulating the Poor: The Functions of Public Welfare*, by Frances Fox Piven and Richard A. Cloward, New York: Random House, 1971, p. 11.
2. Others, presumably more sedate, were placed aboard Ships of Fools.
3. Michel Foucault, *Madness and Civilization. A History of Insanity In The Age of Reason*, translated by Richard Howard, New York: Random House, 1965, p. 81.
4. *Ibid.*, p. 68.
5. *Ibid.*
6. France had over 2,000 registered lepers in 1226. There were leper colonies

commonly incarcerated with criminals, because the distinction between them was blurred and because the two categories of individuals evoked similar attitudes of apprehension in the public.

In 1656, by royal decree, the Hôpital Général opened in Paris and, a few years later, had 6,000 inmates. In 1676, another royal decree ordered every city in France to have an Hôpital Général. In North America, the first institutions for the insane were to be found in Quebec in the seventeenth century under Catholic supervision. However, their role was very limited, mainly because of their small size and because their clientele consisted predominantly of upper-class females.[7] In 1717, Monsignor de St.-Vallier ordered six "lodges" built on the grounds of the Quebec Hôpital Général for insane persons who were dangerous. It was only in 1801 that the government made a token gesture toward the treatment of emotional problems by allocating meager funds for this purpose to the hôpitaux généraux of Montreal, Quebec, and Trois-Rivières.[8]

After the French Revolution, as a consequence of new democratic and liberal attitudes (and of scientific developments in other spheres), the treatment accorded the insane became relatively humane; their disorders were for the first time seen as subject to cure. The field of medicine became directly involved.[9] Phillippe Pinel unchained the inmates at major French institutions in 1793 and contributed to the development of a new form of therapy—moral treatment—along with Vincenzo Chiarugi in

---

throughout Europe until the seventeenth century, at which time only a few known lepers were left and were centralized in two or three institutions.

7. J. Ivan Williams *et al.*, "Mental Health and Illness in Canada," in *Deviant Behaviour and Societal Reaction*, edited by Craig L. Boydell *et al.*, Toronto: Holt, Rinehart and Winston, 1972, p. 400.

8. F. Harvey, "Préléminaires à une sociologie historique des maladies mentales au Québec," *Recherches Sociographiques*, 16, 1975, pp. 113-117.

9. However, the definition of medicine has to be placed within the context of these earlier centuries. For instance, in the United States, in the late 1700's and early 1800's, only approximately ten percent of all practitioners had a medical degree. The others were self-made men, many charlatans. Norman Dain, *Concepts of Insanity in the United States 1759-1865*, New Brunswick, N.J.: Rutgers University Press, 1964, p. 25.

Italy, William Tuke in England, and Benjamin Rush in the United States.[10]

Several developments led to new neurological and moral approaches to mental illness. Discoveries in the physical sciences as well as those in physiology and medicine were important contributing factors, as were the general trends towards experimentation and scientific optimism.[11] Insanity gradually came to be linked to brain damage rather than to sin or divine will and, as such, was believed to be a readily curable disease.[12] But, of even greater relevance in light of current trends, was the emphasis which moral treatment placed on the effect of environment—although environment was defined somewhat differently than in present-day conceptions. Emotions of various sorts, such as bereavement, guilt, febrile intellectual concentration, romantic disappointment, and pressure caused by poverty and family stress were seen as impacting on the highly malleable brain. This susceptibility to environmental stimuli meant that a parallel factor could be applied in order to erase or modify pathological conditions. The environment of the afflicted was therefore manipulated—by *removing* the persons from it and placing them in a planned environment.[13]

In the United States, asylums were created which embodied carefully planned regimes. Directed by medical superintendents, they were in theory ruled along humanitarian principles; gone were the restraints, the physical chastisements, and the general filth and bedlam of previous institutions.[14] "Many current therapeutic techniques—open hospitals, non-restraint, and individual care in small institutions—are in effect a reintroduction of the moral treatment of the mid-nineteenth

10. Ruth B. Caplan, *Psychiatry and the Community in Nineteenth-Century America*, New York: Basic Books, 1969.
11. Dain, *op. cit.*, p. 12.
12. Caplan, *op. cit.*, p. 4.
13. This approach bears an interestingly close relation to present emphases on changing the environmental stimuli around the mentally disturbed.
14. The Association of Medical Superintendents of American Institutions for the Insane became later the American Medico-Psychological Association and, finally, the American Psychiatric Association.

century."[15] Discipline and a regular routine of daily activities as well as work were essential elements of this approach. This regimentation within institutions could be found not only in asylums, but in penitentiaries and in workhouses for the poor.[16]

Although Canadian "psychiatry" of the time had its roots in the British system, it was nevertheless heavily influenced by events taking place in the United States. The asylums for "lunatics"[17] built in Canada at first resembled the British county asylums, but their administration was more of the American type with, for instance, medical superintendents.[18] Asylums in Quebec were of a different nature; patients were under the care of religious orders and treatment was influenced by the French tradition.[19]

Although there was enthusiasm regarding the new approach to mental illness, it is probably accurate to say that this enthusiasm was found predominantly among the educated. Unless affected by the illness of a friend or relative, most people probably gave little thought to the matter and remained influenced by biblical concepts of insanity as "demoniacal possession"—to be treated accordingly.[20] Subsequent phases of the treatment of the insane did not always unfold within a progressive framework. Indeed, much regression occurred in subsequent decades (the late 1800's and early 1900's). There was a return to a conception of insanity as primarily hereditary and, therefore, incurable, as well as to mere custodial care. There was a temporary deterioration in the quality of the care dispensed to the emotionally disturbed, so much so that, in the 1880's, there was public concern about the brutal treatment received by inmates, a phenomenon that has recurred up to the

15. Dain, *op. cit.*, p. xiii.

16. David J. Rothman, *The Discovery of the Asylum*, Boston: Little, Brown and Co., 1971.

17. The first Canadian census of "lunatics" was taken for the years 1851-52. Alex Richman, *Psychiatric Care in Canada: Extent and Results*, Royal Commission on Health Services, Ottawa: Queen's Printer, 1966, p. 24.

18. D.G. McKerracher, *Trends in Psychiatric Care*, Royal Commission on Health Services, Ottawa: Queen's Printer, 1966, p.5.

19. *Ibid.*, p. 6.

20. Dain, *op. cit.*, p. 43.

present day.[21] Nevertheless, in spite of regressions, the nine-teenth-century approach to mental disorder had definitely entered the modern era, and was linked to other ideologies regarding social problems in general.[22]

CASE II: POVERTY

An historical parallel to the above developments can be drawn with regard to the poor. Not only are there striking similarities between the treatment of the mad and that of the impoverished, but again the cyclical nature of ideologies and approaches to social problems is apparent and revealing. As will be seen, our current system of welfare (and certain related ideologies) can be traced back to Elizabethan Poor Law.[23]

Although, according to medieval law, the destitute had a right to assistance, and the better-off a duty to provide it, the main emphasis was still placed on individual sins or faults, rather than on social factors as the cause of poverty.[24] (The same was true for mental disorder.) In 1388, English beggars who were adjudged able to work were subject to punishment, and the first Law of Settlement allowed those unable to work to beg only within their parishes of residence or of origin, thereby making paupers subject to banishment from parishes to which they might have migrated. Since charity was dispensed locally, and this law was variously interpreted, the requirement had far-reaching consequences.

21. Caplan, *op. cit.*
22. The turmoil in approaches to mental disorder continues today, as will be seen in subsequent chapters. An important recounting of contemporary conflicts as they affect actual social policies can be seen in Francoise Boudreau, "The Quebec Psychiatric System in Transition: A Case Study in Psychopolitics," *Canadian Review of Sociology and Anthropology*, 17, 1980, pp. 122-137. See also A. Vinet, "La vie quotidienne dans un asile Québécois," *Recherches Sociographiques*, 16, 1975, pp. 85-112.
23. Lawrence M. Friedman, *Government and Slum Housing: A Century of Frustration*, Chicago: Rand McNally, 1968.
24. Blanche D. Coll, *Perspectives in Public Welfare: A History*, Washington: United States Department of Health, Education and Welfare, 1969, p. 2.

In the 1500's, some time after the great plague known as the Black Death, and following widespread looting, vagrancy, and criminality, including spectacular food riots, there was a shift in public and official opinion regarding the treatment of the poor. Slowly, poverty came to be regarded as a form of crime, at least for those who were considered able to work.[25] Beggars, therefore, were frequently treated as criminals; in 1532, the Parliament of Paris decided to arrest beggars and force them to work in the sewers of the city, chained in pairs.[26] A very similar law was enacted by the German emperor in the same period.[27] But the economic situation was exacerbated by wars, and when Henry IV began the siege of Paris, there were more than 30,000 beggars in a population of approximately 100,000.[28] During those decades, beggars were routinely corralled by archers and forced into various institutions, where they were isolated from the rest of the population and at times conscripted to work.

In England, a severe economic depression began in 1594, and in certain counties bread riots erupted as famine threatened. During the first half of the sixteenth century, Henry VIII had destroyed many monasteries and abbeys that previously offered some relief to the poor.[29] This background led to Elizabeth's *Poor Law* of 1597-1601, the first completely secular and comprehensive legislative action on the problem. The Poor Law was progressive for its time but, because of the population's fear of insurrections, it was frequently confused in application with the Vagrancy Acts, and led to harsh treatment of paupers. The Poor Law served as a model for those laws that developed in the colonies, including Canada, and later in the independent United States. And, once again, the subsequent Settlement Acts of 1662 specified that the poor could be helped only within their own parishes, thereby in effect nullifying many of the potential benefits of the Poor Law.

---

25. *Ibid.*, p. 4.
26. Foucault, *op. cit.*, p. 47.
27. Sidney and Beatrice Webb, *English Poor Law History, Part I. The Old Poor Law*, Hamden, Conn.: Anchor Books, 1963, p. 32.
28. *Ibid.*
29. McKerracher, *op. cit.*, p. 148.

The problem of poverty was not the lot of the Old World countries only. Boston already had an almshouse in 1664 and New York established one in 1700 for those cases that could not be helped within their families. Similarly, Catholic charities and related small institutions also existed in Quebec (or New France) in the seventeenth century. The restrictive effects of the English Settlement Acts appeared only later in the colonies, when the problem of pauperism became more acute, both numerically and economically. Just as the asylums had spread across the United States in the 1820's and 1830's under the reform of "moral treatment," so too almshouses spread as well, armed with the same treatment ideology of removal of the poor from the community while providing them with surroundings fostering discipline, work, and moral uplifting in the hope of rehabilitation. Although the effects of certain deleterious social circumstances on the lives of the poor were recognized by an enlightened minority (the Society for the Prevention of Pauperism already existed), there was still a strong tendency to blame the poor themselves for their condition, and such vices as drinking were stressed as the source of all of their misfortunes.

The problem of the poor was related not only to ideology but to the economic situation of the society as a whole. For instance, although the Poor Law was profusely debated in the United States in the years of scarcity beginning in 1795, the debate lost some of its urgency in the years between the end of scarcity and 1815.[30] In England, a continued increase in expenses incurred for the care of the poor as well as dangers of rural insurrection certainly acted as spurs to legislative rethinking.[31]

Although it is impossible to pinpoint precisely the time when the issue of "poverty amid plenty" moved onto center stage, the publication of Robert Hunter's Poverty in 1904 is considered a convenient point of departure.[32] The issue had already been debated for several years; in 1900, the sociologist William

30. J.R. Poynter, Society and Pauperism: English Ideas on Poor Relief, 1795-1834, Toronto: University of Toronto Press, 1969, p. 186.
31. Sidney and Beatrice Webb, English Local Government: English Poor Law History, Part I. New York: Longmans, Green, 1927, p. 417.
32. Coll, op. cit., p. 64.

Graham Sumner could be quoted on this matter in sentences that remind us in strange ways of discussions on welfare taking place in the 1970's and 1980's:

> The humanitarians, philanthropists, and reformers ... in their eagerness to recommend the less fortunate classes to pity and consideration forget all about the rights of other classes ... When I have read certain of these discussions I have thought that it must be quite disreputable to be respectable, quite dishonest to own property, quite unjust to go one's way and earn one's own living, and that the only admirable person was the good-for-nothing. The man who by his own effort raises himself above poverty appears, in these discussions, to be of no account. The man who has done nothing to raise himself above poverty finds that the social doctors flock about him, bringing the capital which they have collected from other classes.[33]

In both Canada and the United States the terrible trauma of the Great Depression of the 1930's acted as a stimulus for dramatic action by federal governments, laying the foundation for the modern welfare state.[34] Piven and Cloward have pointed out the cyclical nature of poor relief in modern societies. They advance considerable evidence for the thesis that only when times are economically harsh—and large numbers of vocal, articulate persons are unemployed—does relief even begin to approach adequacy.[35] In prosperous times, conditions of welfare are tightened and provisions are made even less generous. Their assertions thus dispute the common liberal assumption that welfare has steadily improved in the twentieth century.

33. This quote from William Graham Sumner's *What Social Classes Owe to Each Other* (New York: Harper and Row, 1900) can be found in *Poverty In The Affluent Society*, edited by Hanna Messner, New York: Harper and Row, 1966, p. 12.
34. A. Finkel, "Origins of the Welfare State in Canada," in *The Canadian State*, edited by L. Panitch, Toronto: University of Toronto Press, 1977. On the ideology of the welfare state, especially as it applies to Canada, see A.W. Djao, "The Welfare State and Its Ideology," in *Economy, Class and Social Reality*, edited by J.A. Fry, Toronto: Butterworths, 1979.
35. Piven and Cloward, *op. cit.*

During the past decade, the problem of poverty has received more attention in Canada, often allied with concerns for particular segments of the impoverished population.[36] A case in point is the multiple afflictions faced by disadvantaged youth as well as disadvantaged single parents, especially mothers.[37]

CULTURAL AND STRUCTURAL TRENDS

The presentation of the above case studies on the development of modern thinking about mental disorder and poverty spurs us to examine the cultural and structural trends in the unfolding of modern attitudes toward social problems in general. Social problems—as a new conceptualization, not a new phenomenon—emerged during the eighteenth and nineteenth centuries as a result of several mutually reinforcing developments. On the structural level, as we will see momentarily, severe stresses were created by industrialization and urbanization. Accompanying these structural transformations were marked changes in social thought on the cultural level: a growing humanitarianism and the rise of middle-class reformers, democratic trends, and a new scientific ideology and secular rationality.[38]

The new order created by industrialization was drastically at variance with existing social arrangements, requiring a completely different style of life for which people were not prepared. It was a pervasive change touching not some few isolated aspects in people's lives, but their complete social condition. And because the new system was everywhere triumphant, the only viable solution was submission and a degree of adaptation.

36. For an excellent collection, see *Poverty in Canada*, edited by John Harp and John R. Hofley, Scarborough, Ont.: Prentice-Hall, 1971. Two hard-hitting books on poverty are Ian Adams et al., *The Real Poverty Report*, Edmonton: Hurtig, 1971 and Ian Adams, *The Poverty Wall*, Toronto: McClelland and Stewart, 1970. See also the Senate of Canada, *Poverty in Canada*, Ottawa: Parliamentary Secretary, 1980, and Donald Caskie, *The Canadian Fact Book on Poverty*, Ottawa: Canadian Council on Social Development, 1979.
37. Canadian Council on Children and Youth, *Admittance Restricted: The Child as Citizen in Canada*, Ottawa: 1978.
38. Jessie Bernard, *Social Problems At Midcentury*, New York: Dryden, 1957, pp. 90-91.

But everything in industrialization was alien: the sheer magnitude of the stresses involved in trying to adapt to this unprecedented situation were incalculable. In addition, industrialization and accompanying urbanization in no way alleviated problems that had plagued the masses for centuries. The proletariat* was now burdened with long working hours, deficient nutrition, poor health, suffocating housing, and unbearable poverty. Emile Zola, the famous French experimental novelist, has given us memorable tableaux of the misery of the newly industrialized populace and of their dysfunctional* coping mechanisms: alcoholism, mental derangement, promiscuity, and brutality, even within the family. In some strange ways, although with obvious differences of detail, his descriptions fit pictures we occasionally see of the most wretched slum dwellers of today. Never before in history had so many people, ostensibly free, toiled under such miserable conditions and within so small and cramped a space.[39] The miseries became blatant and could not be hidden:

Commission after commission in Britain documented the inhuman conditions under which people lived in factory towns and city slums. The culture of these new industrial slums was as alien to outsiders as the culture of a distant African tribe. Indeed, after half a century of reform legislation, one passionate observer ... wrote a book describing "darkest England," comparing it with the "darkest Africa" on which Stanley had just reported.[40]

Alongside this widespread misery, political revolutions took place in Europe, first in France, then a half century later throughout the entire continent, in which the masses not only played a major role but also called attention to themselves as human beings rather than as members of a lower species. The suffering of the masses became socially visible and, for some people in the elite structure, worth paying attention to. A new

---

39. See Michael Cross, *The Workingman in the Nineteenth Century*, Toronto: Oxford University Press (Readings in Canadian Social History Series), 1974.
40. Bernard (*op. cit.* p. 91) is referring to the founder of the Salvation Army, General William Booth, who wrote *In Darkest England*, published in 1890.

ideological orientation of humanitarianism arose in the eighteenth century which encouraged condemnation of the situation. In contrast to earlier ideas of the *inevitability* of poverty for the lowly masses, the proletariat's suffering became bona fide human suffering, unnecessary and in urgent need of a solution.

Another element in the development of the notion of social problems was the emergence of middle-class reformers who did not themselves suffer from the conditions they defined as problematic:

> The newly enriched middle classes largely determined the intellectual climate of the eighteenth century, although their accession to power came somewhat later. The middle classes unlike the nobles were trained for peace and not for wars; they were not even accustomed to the blood of the hunting field.[41]

Middle-class reformers were guided by a humanitarian rationalist viewpoint, and were themselves a distinct social category—the very creations of this new industrial order and its greatest beneficiaries—at the confluence between the afflicted classes and the upper classes responsible for the situation through exploitation and legislation. Members of the middle class, not being completely involved with either of the two extreme class positions, could grasp the situation from a relatively detached perspective. The reformers arising from their ranks were able to achieve a view of the bottom as well as the top. Democracy was also a new product of these ages, thereby making all fellow citizens equal, at least in legalistic theory.[42] As we saw earlier, this meant that the suffering of the "low" classes could at last be recognized as a problem and not as the inevitable affliction of those "born to suffer."

41. Crane Brinton, "Humanitarianism," in *Encyclopedia of the Social Sciences*, New York: Macmillan, 1932, vol. 7, pp. 544-548.
42. For a sense of how hotly debatable the emerging doctrines of legal equality and universal suffrage were in the 1800's, see Christopher Kent, *Brains and Numbers: Elitism, Comtism, and Democracy in Mid-Victorian England*, Toronto: University of Toronto Press, 1978.

Along with the new drive toward humanitarian reform, a scientific value system and a new conception of progress emerged from the successes of the physical sciences. Secular rationalism, or the secularization of formerly sacred thought, was a development that paralleled or preceded the development of a scientific orientation. One effect of this development was that people no longer viewed the social order as one dictated by divine will and therefore irremediable. This new perception of the situation allowed for the rise of reformers and of social movements,* a phenomenon previously incompatible with the vision of an unalterable status quo.[43] The successes of the natural sciences and the secularization of thought led intellectuals to consider applying the principles of science to the human realm as well. In the seventeenth and eighteenth centuries, scientific developments led to a more optimistic and active view of humanity, and to the possibility of applying scientific rules for universal betterment.

The period of which we are speaking, particularly its earlier part in the late 1700's, saw the development of a phenomenal faith in human progress. Surrounded by human misery, the writers of the period were nonetheless in virtual awe of the intellectual accomplishments which had been achieved so recently in the sciences and humanities. Extrapolating into the future they foresaw endless improvement. The period has sometimes been termed the "Age of Reason" by historians of social thought, not because the age was so reasonable in the conduct of human affairs but because there was such a great *faith* in the powers of reason. (The unreasoning side of the human psyche was yet to be unveiled by Freud and others.)[44] The idea of progress found such proponents in this period as the Marquis de Condorcet who, in 1793, wrote his *Outline of an*

43. Rudolph Heberle, "Social Movements," in *International Encyclopedia of the Social Sciences*, New York: Crowell, Collier and Macmillan, 1968, vol. 14, p. 440. As an example of the hold of the sacred, it was once believed that the "trinity" of classes on earth—at that time the nobility, the clergy, and the peasantry—was a reflection of the Trinity in Heaven, showing the inevitability and rightness of such an arrangement. Obviously, such beliefs or justifications of the status quo were often fatal to any reasoned questioning of the prevailing social structure.
44. See Michael Creal, *The Idea of Progress*, Agincourt, Ont.: Macmillan, 1970.

Historical Picture of the Progress of the Human Mind. Charac-
teristically, we find these lines: "nature has assigned no limit to
the perfecting of the human faculties, that the perfectibility of
man is truly infinite."[45] Humanitarianism and democratic phi-
losophies are evident in Condorcet's discussion of the three
types of inequality he perceived to exist within a nation: the
inequality of wealth, that of a man of assured income as
opposed to a man whose income depends on his ability to work,
and that of the differential education given to children. Saint-
Simon was an equally fervent advocate of the idea of progress.
"He held that the rapid transformation of social and economic
conditions which was being brought about by the scientific and
industrial revolutions necessitated the creation of a real science
of social progress, based upon thoroughly positive [scientific]
grounds."[46] While for him this was *la science politique*, it fell to
his disciple, Auguste Comte, to call it *sociologie*.[47]

SOCIAL SCIENCE AND SOCIAL PROBLEMS

We thus have the timely beginning of the social sciences.[48]
Social science associations, supplying the transition from the
amateur to professionalism, were created in England (1857), in
France (1862), and in the United States (1865). One purpose of
these early associations was to find ways through scientific

45. As quoted in Howard Becker and Harry Elmer Barnes, *Social Thought
From Lore to Science*, third edition, New York: Dover, 1961, p. 474. For an
overview of the extreme optimism of the period see Robert Nisbet, *History of
the Idea of Progress*, New York: Basic Books, 1980.
46. Becker and Barnes, *ibid.*, p. 501.
47. For detailed discussions of early sociological theories, see excellent
treatments in Becker and Barnes, *ibid.*, and Pitirim Sorokin, *Contemporary
Sociological Theories*, New York: Harper, 1928. For a more detailed discussion
of the intellectual ferment in the French capital in this era (Condorcet, Saint-
Simon, Comte, and others) see Frank Manuel, *The Prophets of Paris*, Cambridge, Mass.: Harvard University Press, 1962.
48. One additional development of the period—which, however, did not
immediately become connected with the social sciences—was the emergence in
the nineteenth century of statistical information of some reliability. For a
discussion of the importance of this development see Chapter 2 of Burkhart
Holzner and John H. Marx, *Knowledge Application: The Knowledge System in
Society*, Boston: Allyn and Bacon, 1979.

means to alleviate the social injustices that were recognized at the time. Conversely, any situation that was felt to be in need of being remedied by middle-class reformers became a social problem. And we have here the beginning of what we discussed in the previous chapter as the social definition aspect of social problems, as well as all the attendant obscurities surrounding what is to be thus defined.

In spite of its early ameliorative emphasis under Saint-Simon and Comte, European sociology developed with considerably less emphasis on social problems than its American counterpart.[49] However, in 1897, the great French sociologist, Emile Durkheim, attacked from this new scientific perspective the problem of suicide. His work is now a classic in sociology, and greatly encouraged the first, slow beginnings of the scientific study of social problems. In the meantime, social problems had already become a matter of academic interest in the United States, although several years had to elapse before a work of great empirical importance was produced.[50] Nevertheless, under the impetus of the now defunct American Association of Social Sciences, courses on social problems were offered in universities and colleges beginning in 1865 and reaching an early peak between 1885 and 1895.[51]

Courses on social problems never acquired such a popularity in Canada, as the establishment of the social sciences took place after the initial ferment was already over in the United States. The first sociology course in English Canada was offered in

49. J. Graham Morgan, "Contextual Factors in the Rise of Academic Sociology in the United States," *Canadian Review of Sociology and Anthropology*, 7, 1970, pp. 159-171. Early criminology developed independently of sociology, and European contributions to the former were considerable. For an excellent treatment of the development of theories of deviance in the nineteenth century see Lynn McDonald, *The Sociology of Law and Order*, Montreal: Book Centre, 1976.

50. Emile Durkheim, *Suicide*, Glencoe, Ill.; Free Press, 1951 (1897). W.E.B. DuBois's study of the Negro in Philadelphia, published in 1899, and Thomas and Znaniecki's study of the Polish peasant in Europe and America, in 1918, are considered the best of the early American studies on social problems.

51. Edwin M. Lemert, "Social Problems," in *International Encyclopedia of the Social Sciences*, 1968, vol. 14, p. 452. For an outstanding overview of the development of professionalism in nineteenth century social science in the United States, see Thomas L. Haskell, *The Emergence of Professional Social Science*, Urbana, Ill.: University of Illinois Press, 1977.

1908. In Quebec, the process took far longer; until the 1950's most written works on social problems and social issues were done by members of the clergy or by intellectuals linked to religious institutions.[52]

We should not convey the erroneous impression that the social sciences in their formative years were unequivocally in favour of active amelioration of social problems. The concept of laissez faire had developed at the hands of the classical economists, Adam Smith and David Ricardo. Ricardo had also formulated the "iron law of wages" which proved, supposedly, that wages of workers could not remain far above the bare subsistence level. Robert Michels formulated a similar "iron law of oligarchy" to show that all organizations eventually became oligarchical. Even the founder of sociology, Auguste Comte, was by no means an unequivocal advocate of reform, and two of the most prominent early sociologists, Sumner (quoted earlier in the chapter) and Spencer, were reactionary. In spite of such countertrends, the thrust of early social science was nonetheless clearly reformative and ameliorationist in character.[53]

Between 1920 and 1950, North American sociologists increasingly abandoned the arena of social problems (except in criminology) and left it to social workers. A major rift developed between the two disciplines, with sociologists viewing social workers merely as "do-gooders" with little sense of academic objectivity, and the latter retaliating in kind by considering sociologists "pseudo-scientists" in ivory towers.[54]

52. M. Fournier and G. Houle, "La sociologie québécoise et son objet: problématiques et débats/Quebec sociology and its object: problematics and debates," *Sociologie et Sociétes*, 12, 1980, pp. 21-44. Other helpful references are: H. Carrier, *Le Sociologue Canadien Léon Gérin, 1863-1951*, Montreal: Bellarmin, 1959; J.-C. Falardeau, *Etienne Parent, 1802-1874*, Montreal: La Presse, 1974; A. Saint-Pierre, *Questions et Oeuvres Sociales Chez Nous*, Montreal: Ecole Sociale Populaire, 1914, and *Le Problème Social*, Montreal: Bibliothèque Canadienne, 1925.
53. For historical accounts of the development of sociology see Becker and Barnes, *op. cit.*; Desmond M. Connor and James E. Curtis, *Sociology and Anthropology in Canada*, Montreal: Canadian Sociology and Anthropology Association, September, 1970; Roscoe C. Hinkle and Gisela Hinkle, *The Development of Modern Sociology*, New York: Random House, 1962.
54. Arnold M. Rose, "History and Sociology of the Study of Social Problems,"

The disaffection of sociologists from social problems resulted from a new ideological commitment to social neutrality, accompanying an emphasis on scientific and objective study (positivism).[55] There was, therefore, a renewed emphasis on developing sociology as a science and, consequently, on studying social phenomena with detachment in order to detect social laws or regularities.

But concern with social problems never entirely disappeared, and in 1952 the Society for the Study of Social Problems was founded by sociologists who believed in the possibility of studying social problems objectively and who wished to return to their earlier emphasis. After a slow beginning this return to the study of social problems gained increasing momentum in the 1960's. However, this resurgence of social problems in the discipline of sociology took place within the framework of new concerns, such as the need for a theory of social problems.[56] The issue of value commitment versus neutrality is still debated and, once again, factions have been created in the field of social problems.[57] Value neutrality has been questioned and social commitment has once more re-entered the scene—as one more example of the cyclical nature of ideologies, even in scientific endeavour.[58] And, related to these new trends was a renewed emphasis on conflict theories and the emergence of the labeling school, as discussed in the next chapter.

---

in *Handbook on the Study of Social Problems*, edited by Erwin O. Smigel, Chicago: Rand McNally, 1971.

55. Lemert, *op. cit.*, p. 453. Rose, *op cit.*, suggests the shift also arose from sociologists' chagrin over their discipline's low academic status.

56. It should not be supposed that the interlude of excessive concern with scientific purity was of no lasting value, even to those sociologists today exclusively preoccupied with social problems. When the discipline returned to its earlier concerns it did so with far greater sophistication in terms of employment of statistics and other positivist research tools.

57. James B. McKee, "Some Observations on the Self-Consciousness of Sociologists," in *The Sociology of Sociology*, edited by Larry T. Reynolds and Janice M. Reynolds, New York: McKay, 1970, p. 102.

58. Very descriptive of new trends is this title: ". . . Who Shall Prepare Himself to the Battle?" by Thomas Ford Hoult, *American Sociologist*, 3, 1968, pp. 3-7. But, most importantly, see Alvin W. Gouldner, "Anti-Minotaur: the Myth of a Value-Free Sociology," *Social Problems*, 9, 1962, pp. 199-213.

SUMMARY

A review of the history of social concerns reveals unmistakably that the conditions we regard today as social problems have not always been so regarded. In fact, modern conceptions of problematic conditions are just that: modern points of view. The central purpose of this chapter has been to provide an overview of the historical development of certain key ideas and, perhaps of even greater importance, to impart a historical perspective to social problems issues.

Two cases studied in the slow evolution of outlook were selected for examination in somewhat greater depth. Mental disorder was regarded at one time as a manifestation of divine wrath, and treatment was bestial because persons so afflicted were regarded as beasts. Conditions improved during the Enlightenment period and very gradually a notion of possible cure began, however naive the treatment seems today. One important notion to be gained here is the cyclical process of reform alternating with the regression to harsh treatment over an extended period of several centuries. Views toward poverty display the same cyclical alternation between charitable periods and periods in which poverty is construed as individual sloth and begging as a crime. The course of poverty legislation can be traced from the Elizabethan Poor Law to the origins of the Welfare State in the Great Depression.

Turning to more general trends in viewpoint, the major transformations in culture and social structure in what historians call the modern and early modern periods have shaped contemporary thinking about social problems. In terms of social structure, the uprooting of millions of farmers and peasants by land enclosure acts, their settlement into squalid teeming city slums, their sixty-hour work week in impersonal black factories—in short the chaos of early industrialization and urbanization—gave a quality and visibility, not previously encountered, to suffering. Early urban revolts, even while unsuccessful, heightened this visibility. The rise of a large middle-class between the traditional elite and peasant-labourers paralleled major cultural developments—in particular, belief in democracy and legal equality. The unparalleled faith in progress throughout much of this period, faith in the power of human rationality and technical achievements, combined with growing democratization to produce a demand for and belief in the possibility of improvement in the life of the common citizen. No longer did mass suffering appear inevitable and unavoidable.

The factors which finally led to the perception of deleterious conditions as social problems and to the questioning of the prevailing order are finely and intricately interwoven. These factors—secular rationalism, scientific ideology, as well as humanitarianism on the ideological level and, on the structural level, industrialization, urbanization, and the rise of a strategically situated middle class—were all in dynamic interrelationship* and were perhaps essential prerequisites to the conceptualization of social problems and, especially, the rational study of such problems.

Finally, material abundance, or the possibility of such in the twentieth century, contributes to the emergence in social consciousness of new problems. As George and Wilding note, when there is no possibility of a solution, a condition is just a fact, not a problem. Thus "poverty only becomes a problem where there are resources available which *could* be used to reduce it. A society has to attain a certain degree of prosperity before it has any sense of a problem of poverty."[59] So too with the inclusion among social problems of conditions related to "malfunctions of roles and status."[60] Problems of mere survival and physical pain are now complemented by psychological pains. "Modern industrial man is probably the most problem-blessed in all history. For, encouraged by a sense of control over nature, he has joined the survival problems of the past to the style of life problems of the present."[61]

59. V. George and P. Wilding, *Motherless Families*, London: Routledge and Kegan Paul, 1972, p. 175.

60. Bernard, *op. cit.*, p. viii.

61.. William R. Burch, Jr., "Images of Future Leisure: Continuities in Changing Expectations," in *The Sociology of the Future*, edited by Wendell Bell and James A. Mau, New York: Russell Sage, 1971, p. 161.

3 Theoretical Approaches to Social Problems

> The Law, in its majestic impartiality, forbids the rich and the poor alike to sleep under bridges, to beg in the streets, and to steal bread.
>
> —Anatole France

A history of the modern concept of social problems is not complete without an examination of the basic theoretical perspectives that have been assumed by different sociologists. There have been at least five widely used theoretical approaches to social problems in sociology. These are, in approximate chronological order of development, social pathology, social disorganization, conflict, deviance, and labeling or reaction theory.[1]

SOCIAL PATHOLOGY

The oldest theoretical perspective concerning social problems is that of social pathology, an approach in widespread use before

---

1. This chapter follows closely the excellent discussion of these approaches in *The Study of Social Problems: Five Perspectives*, edited by Earl Rubington and Martin Weinberg, New York: Oxford University Press, 1971. For a critical view of the failure of these approaches with respect to the process of collective definition, see Herbert Blumer, "Social Problems as Collective Behavior," *Social Problems*, 8, 1971, pp. 298-306.

World War I. In the past two decades the notion has been revitalized, with major changes, in conjunction with widespread social unrest and ideological turmoil.

Social pathology is an extension of the biological perspective into sociology in the sense that society is equated with an organism. Under the organic analogy, society is seen as healthy or sickly, or as functioning normally or abnormally. It is the task of the sociologist to detect and cure the sickness—under this medical model he is a "social pathologist."

In the early version of this perspective (with which the school is usually associated), the emphasis was on defective individuals as the cause of most social problems. Specific persons were singled out, and the social pathologist commonly adopted a position of moral outrage toward these people which contrasted poorly with his accompanying attitude that they were sick or inherently defective. The solution called for such individuals to adjust themselves to a norm of what the diagnostician considered healthy.

There has been a shift of focus between the first wave of social pathology, described above, and the current version, in the sense that it is now the system that is seen as unhealthy—again, a biological analogy. And the afflicted individuals in that society are now seen as its victims rather than as its sick accompaniments, as was the case in the earlier interpretation. This means that treatment of the problem is often viewed as requiring society-wide changes, within a political framework, rather than on an individual basis, with no commitment in the recent version to impose conformity on people who are now considered the "victims."[2] In the United States, political assassinations and other acts of violence have been followed by soul searching in the mass media and by such captions as "Is our society sick?" Individuals are seen by such contemporary social pathologists as basically good; it is society's institutions which are bad, which corrupt the individual, and which need to be changed or eradicated.

2. However, even today there remain perspectives which see the principal cause as individually based—from socialization and cultural defects—and prescribe treatment in terms of "breaking the cycle" of poverty, excessive procreation, and so on.

An interesting usage of the concept of social pathology is Kavolis's attempt to present a framework for a viable cross-cultural analysis of social problems.[3] According to this perspective, pathological behaviour is that which is destructive. Cross-cultural research should therefore focus on two subjects: (a) It should distinguish what is truly pathological behaviour, that is, self-directed and other-directed destructiveness (destruction of life, health, or sense of personal identity), from what is merely deviance relative to a particular set of norms. Kavolis is, of course, suggesting the possibility of universal human needs, and also of universal ways of inhibiting or preventing the fulfillment of these needs. (b) Cross-cultural research should also study the structural and cultural arrangements that give or will give rise to these pathological results, including organized pathology such as wars and concentration camps.[4]

In the wake of subsequent social developments, the traditional social pathology approach of the early 1900's lost much of its appeal. There was always very little doubt as to what constituted a healthy organism, physically speaking, but the usefulness of the analogy was very doubtful when applied to "moral health," even at the level of the individual.[5] And as for what a healthy society looked like, there came to be less and less agreement on the subject.

The growth of cultural relativity in sociology ... together with the general questioning of paramount American values that was generated by the great depression of the 1930's and by foreign revolutions, put an end to social pathology as a viable perspective on social problems.... Many of the phenomena that had long been the subject matter of social problems or social pathology now were postulated as symptoms or products of such processes as uneven cultural

3. Vytautas Kavolis, *Comparative Perspectives on Social Problems*, Boston: Little, Brown, 1969.
4. He views his framework as different from that of earlier social pathologists and, as such, believes that C. Wright Mills's major criticism of them (to be discussed) does not apply to his variation.
5. Friedrich Nietzsche, *Beyond Good and Evil*, Chicago: Henry Regnery, 1955 (1885), p. 105.

development, conflict, dissensus, and dialectical change.
Taken together, these processes mean social disorganization.[6]

SOCIAL DISORGANIZATION

By the 1920's, the steady growth of urbanization, immigration, and industrialization in the United States had created a set of social problems for which it was obvious that the orientations provided by the traditional social pathology model were inadequate. Why immigrants who had been well adjusted in the old society would again and again become involved with social problems in American society was not a problem stemming from individual pathology. The answer to this question, which began to emerge from the Chicago School of sociology, was termed social disorganization.[7]

As Rubington and Weinberg put it,

Organization implies, firstly, a whole [society] whose parts
are in some ordered relationship to one another, and, then,
secondarily, the negative concept of disorganization. In the
case of disorganization, the various parts which make up the
whole are out of phase with one another. As such they do not
work well together, if at all. Central to the entire conception
. . . is the notion of rules. Rules define not only the different
parts of society but how they will join together.[8]

Social disorganization, then, occurs when the rules or norms are inadequate in some respect.

Three basic forms of inadequacy with respect to norms have been examined as factors in the development of social problems. *Normlessness* occurs when, on a large scale, persons perceive

6. Edwin Lemert, "Social Problems," *International Encyclopedia of the Social Sciences*, New York: Crowell, Collier and Macmillan, 1968, vol. 14, p. 455.
7. Thomas and Znaniecki are credited with developing the concept of social disorganization. William I. Thomas and Florian Znaniecki, *The Polish Peasant in Europe and America*, two-volume edition, New York: Dover, 1958 (first published in 1918).
8. Rubington and Weinberg, *op. cit.*, p. 49, italics added. The concept of social organization was not a new one in sociology; only its application to social problems was novel.

no guiding rules to govern their behaviour under prevailing circumstances. *Culture conflict* is in many ways the opposite problem: it occurs when, on a large scale, two or more cultures which exert some influence over individuals provide them with too many rules, some of which are in conflict. Finally, *normative breakdown* occurs if, on a massive scale, conformity to the rules no longer brings the usual rewards, or perhaps even leads to consistently negative results.[9] These are the basic dynamics out of which a number of more specific situations are seen as leading to social problems.

Three widely noted occasions of social disorganization may be mentioned at this point. First, culture conflict can occur for large numbers of people under a situation of extensive immigration, or of migration from rural to urban areas. It can also systematically affect their offspring, caught between the traditional ways of their parents and the rules of the host society. Such generational conflicts between immigrant parents and their children are especially acute during the teenage years.

A second important occasion for social disorganization is the conquest of one society by another, with the resulting intrusion of a very different social structure and culture—an instance of both culture conflict and normative breakdown. This is especially relevant when far-reaching acculturation* is required as a result of the colonization of a simpler society by one more complex—as happened throughout Africa, to the Indian and the Inuit in America, and as is still happening in other parts of the world. For instance, there is currently much concern over the disorganizing effects on South American Indian tribes of a rapid and haphazard acculturation forced upon them by economic encroachment upon their native habitat.

A third focus of considerable attention was the notion that different parts of a culture change at different rates. (In particular, there was the idea that the material culture—technology—changes faster than the non-material.) Because of this difference, aspects of a culture formerly in phase with one another can become increasingly disharmonious, and normative breakdown can occur. This is what Ogburn, the most

9. We are indebted to Rubington and Weinberg, *op. cit.*, for this classification.

famous investigator of the problem, called "*cultural lag*."[10] Cultural lag would, of course, be most common in a situation of rapid social or technological change, such as that which took place during the first phases of industrialization in Great Britain. There is concern about possible social disorganization among technological Western societies as a consequence of the ever-increasing pace of social and cultural change, the lag that may result between socialization content and reality, and the possibility of broken interpersonal networks.[11]

Indicators of whether social disorganization is taking place include widespread violence of various types, conflicts between segments of the society, apathy, and anomie,* all of which can exist simultaneously within a society. There are various degrees of social disorganization, and it is likely that every society experiences the phenomenon to some extent. Also, the more complex and differentiated a society, the greater is the likelihood that it will encounter disorganization on a large scale as consensus becomes more difficult to attain and subsystems work at cross-purposes. Lack of social disorganization does not necessarily imply a static society in spite of the fact that many theoreticians have made it synonymous with the status quo, or that others define social disorganization as a consequence of change. As more sophisticated treatments have indicated, a society need not be static to be organized and integrated.

CONFLICT THEORY

Although there is a long history of sociologists who have called themselves conflict theorists, early discussions about social problems in America were curiously devoid of references to intentional conflict over competing ideals.[12] (To avoid confusion over terminology, we should be clear that the kind of self-

10. William F. Ogburn, *Social Change*, New York; Heubsch, 1922.
11. For an excellent discussion of the increasingly transient nature of personal relations, see Alvin Toffler's *Future Shock*, New York: Bantam Books, 1970. His discussion of the consequences of increasingly rapid social change is also important from the standpoint of social disorganization.
12. This deficiency is curious in view of the extensive comments on social problems by Marxists in the latter half of the nineteenth century. This

conscious and organized conflict between advocates of opposing values which is now being discussed is quite distinct from
the pathetic confusion caused by culture conflict—despite the
similarity of labels.) It took the myriad struggles of the 1930's to
bring the older conflict theories into the arena of social problems. Louis Wirth and C. Wright Mills, in papers discussed
elsewhere in this book,[13] described the shortcomings of social
pathology and social disorganization; Richard Fuller laid down
the fundamentals of a conflict theory of social problems in a
series of papers published in the late 1930's.[14]

Conflict theory examines social problems from the viewpoint
of a struggle within society between more-or-less inherently
opposed faction.[15] Two or more groups uphold different and
opposing values, and these groups have to interact to a certain
degree because of mutual interdependence. (The contemporary
religious situation in Northern Ireland is an excellent case in
point.) The tension, mutual mistrust, and divergent values of
the groups generate violence, which per se intensifies the
conflict as well as becoming problematic in itself. The underlying cause of the conflict is seen as a divergence of valus, which,
when taken with the growing awareness of these value differences among the members of the groups, becomes an organized
struggle within a society.

Although conflict theorists could conceivably stop here, they
also typically posit an *inherent conflict* between groups with
divergent vested interests, or between those with a self-interest

---

tradition, however, remained relatively isolated from American social science
until much later.

13. Louis Wirth, "Ideological Aspects of Social Disorganization," *American
Sociological Review*, 5, 1940, pp. 472-482; C. Wright Mills, "The Professional
Ideology of Social Pathologists," in his *Power, Politics, and People*, New York:
Oxford University Press, 1963 (1942 original), pp. 525-552.

14. For example, see Richard C. Fuller, "Sociological Theory and Social
Problems," *Social Forces*, 15, 1937, pp. 496-502.

15. Horton sees two types of conflict theory: the type discussed here and what
most writers have termed culture conflict. See John Horton, "Order and
Conflict Theories of Social Problems," *American Journal of Sociology*, 71,
1966, pp. 701-713. See John Hagan's mistitled work, *The Disreputable Pleasures*, Toronto: McGraw-Hill Ryerson, 1977, for an excellent and systematic
contrasting of order and conflict theories.

in maintaining the status quo and those with an interest in changing it. Since it describes social problems in terms of a clash of self-interest—blacks versus whites, rich versus poor—this approach might also be considered an "interest theory" of social problems.[16] The model can be applied to inter-group relations, including gender relations, social inequality, poverty, and, to some extent, criminality and mental illness.

Although its essential features were laid down in the 1930's, the conflict approach to social problems underwent something of an eclipse in subsequent years.[17] The perspective has received increasing attention since the mid-1960's, as the hitherto automatically accepted standards and values of the middle class have undergone challenges from racial and ethnic cultural nationalism. Moreover, the women's movement has challenged traditional male domination, both structurally and normatively.[18] The "other side's" values have now been defended as legitimate, and social problems have increasingly taken on the appearance of a struggle between self-conscious groups.[19]

The conflict perspective on the sources of social problems bears a close affinity to conflict interpretations of the origins of law. The issue of whether the sources of criminal law are based on a widespread *consensus* in society or, conversely, on the triumph of more powerful sectors over less powerful in getting their notions embedded in law (a *conflict* interpretation) is discussed in Chapters 4 and 5.[20]

16. See Ralf Dahrendorf, *Class and Class Conflict in Industrial Society*, Stanford: Stanford University Press, 1959, Chapters 5 and 6.
17. For an insightful interpretation of the adherence of sociologists to specific doctrines of social problems in terms of outside events of the day (a sociology of knowledge perspective), see Rubington and Weinberg, *op. cit.* They "parallel" their discussions of each perspective with descriptions of the contemporaneous developments in the external world.
18. For the situation in Canada, see A.-M. Ambert, *Sex Structure*, second edition, revised and expanded, Toronto: Longman Canada, 1976.
19. For this reason some prefer to speak of social issues rather than social problems in order to highlight the disagreement over whether a particular condition represents a "problem." See Sidney M. Willhelm, "Elites, Scholars, and Sociologists," *Catalyst*, 2, 1966, pp. 1-10. For significant insights on the *naming* of a problem (e.g., we have a problem of poverty, not a problem of wealth), see William Ryan, *Blaming the Victim*, New York: Vintage Books, 1971.
20. For an excellent example of a conflict interpretation see M.R. Goode, "Law

DEVIANCE

Although social disorganization and conflict theories made significant advances in explaining why certain situations were more likely to produce social problems, they were inadequate as explanations of why *specific individuals* embarked on particular courses of action. Why, for instance, did some persons in conditions of conflict or social disorganization choose a course of anti-social behaviour and others in the same situation choose a different course? What was needed to answer this question was a theory of individual action. Social pathology had attempted to provide such a theory, but its early conceptions of inherited incompetence and later theories of abnormal psychology could not account for more than a fraction of contra-normative acts. Deviance theories, arising in the 1930's and steadily maturing in later decades, attempted to fill the gap.

Deviance means a departure from the norms regulating the behaviour of persons occupying certain positions (role-status sets*). Deviance is relative to roles and pertains to norms, that is, blueprints for behaviour in certain situations. For instance, it is considered appropriate to take morphine when under medical care but it is considered deviant to take it as part of one's daily routine. One situation refers to the role of the sick and the other to roles not seen as requiring morphine, such as the role of student. Deviance is also relative to the observer, as the example illustrates. When social problems are discussed within the deviance framework, we are faced with a problem of definition: what is deviant behaviour, and who decides what it is? One may be tempted to say that, since deviance involves the breaking or evading of norms, deciding what is deviant may be less of a problem than deciding what is a social problem. But, since some deviations are applauded (e.g., scientific discoveries), the important question is one of deciding which deviances are harmful. We will come back to this question when we discuss the labeling perspective.

Reform Commission of Canada—Political Ideology of Criminal Process Reform," *Canadian Bar Review*, 1976, pp. 653-674.

While social disorganization involves a technical failure of the system, deviance involves an individual phenomenon. It can be said that social disorganization and deviance are dynamically interrelated: large-scale deviance will lead to social disorganization and, in turn, social disorganization constitutes a favourable breeding ground for the evolution of various types of deviant activity.[21] As Merton explains, most social problems could be explored by either approach, although each social problem will differ in the extent to which one approach is causally valid.[22]

Two streams of development can be seen for theories of deviance, both centering around the principles of social learning. One is concerned with the individual's contacts with carriers of deviant and conventional ideas; the other deals with the conditions which facilitate the learning of one set of these ideas or the other. The theory of *differential association*, first put forth by Sutherland in 1939, explicitly declares deviance to be a result of ordinary learning processes, and claims that differences between individuals in terms of behaviour are due to the frequency, duration, temporal priority, and intensity of their contacts with deviant and conventional persons.[23] But while this theory can explain that kind of deviance which results from involuntary contacts, it fails to consider that many social contacts are voluntary, and it neglects to explain just why persons choose certain others with whom to have these voluntary contacts. Merton's *anomie theory*[24] and Cohen's later

21. "Deviation originates from permutations of choice by individuals motivated by culturally given ends and confronted with means of varying accessibility" (Lemert, *op. cit.*, 1968, p. 457).
22. Robert K. Merton, "Social Problems and Sociological Theory," in *Contemporary Social Problems*, third edition, edited by Robert K. Merton and Robert Nisbet, New York: Harcourt, Brace, Jovanovich, 1971, p. 819.
23. Edwin H. Sutherland, *Principles of Criminology*, Philadelphia: Lippincott, 1939.
24. Robert K. Merton, "Social Structure and Anomie," *American Sociological Review*, 3, 1939, pp. 672-682. Although the Mertonian framework has been most frequently applied to criminality, it is also relevant to other forms of deviance. For example,it can be applied to school withdrawal: Eigil Pedersen and Kenneth Etheridge, "Conformist and Deviant Behaviour in High School: The Merton Typology Adapted to an Educational Context," *Canadian Review of Sociology and Anthropology*, 7, 1970, pp. 70-82.

work on the delinquent response[25] provide the structural conditions which lead to preferences for certain kinds of associations with other people. Merton shows how the strain between accepting culturally valued ends or goals and lacking socially approved means to obtain these ends can lead to a search for "innovative" (illicit) means. Cohen explicitly examines the factors behind the emergence of deviant subcultures, in which persons with common frustrations slowly evolve a more gratifying set of shared, deviant outlooks. Cloward and Ohlin's theory of differential legitimate and illegitimate opportunity is a synthesis of Sutherland and Merton.[26]

As can perhaps be sensed from this brief overview, one of the most satisfying aspects of the deviance perspective has been the growth and transformation of earlier theories on the basis of empirical research—a virtue not found to the same extent in earlier perspectives. In its most sophisticated form, deviant behaviour is seen as basically a result of a particular set of learning experiences. Not only different personal associations, but the availability of role models who advocate deviance, and, finally, the provision of rationalizing viewpoints are important. These, in turn, tend to be available in subcultures which emerge when large numbers of persons experience similar strains between cultural expectations and social reality.

LABELING

The prominence of the deviance perspective has made it the recipient of numerous critiques, prominently a self-criticism by Sutherland[27] and a symposium by Clinard on Merton's anomie theory.[28] As recognition increases of the difficulties involved in

25. Albert K. Cohen, *Delinquent Boys*, New York: Free Press, 1955.
26. Cohen's work, and that of Cloward and Ohlin, are directed toward building a theory of deviant (delinquent) subcultures, but they nonetheless fit in closely with the question of individual deviance. Richard A. Cloward and Lloyd E. Ohlin, *Delinquency and Opportunity*, New York: Free Press, 1970.
27. Edwin H. Sutherland, "Differential Association: Theory and Fact," in *The Sutherland Papers*, edited by Albert Cohen *et al.*, Bloomington: Indiana University Press, 1956, pp. 30-41.
28. Marshall B. Clinard, *Anomie and Deviant Behavior: A Discussion and*

understanding the causes of deviance, theoretical interests have shifted. Recent interest has centered around the influence of society's mechanisms of social control* on the incidence and nature of its social problems. Inasmuch as contemporary sociologists tend to be more critical of existing social arrangements than they were in the past, it is perhaps only natural that institutions of social control (the police, the courts, corrections, mental health bureaus, welfare agencies) are seen as inadvertently worsening some of the very problems they attempt to control. This emphasis upon the unintended deleterious consequences of formal agencies of social control* has led to the development of a *reaction theory*, or, as it is more commonly termed, *labeling theory*.

In earlier theoretical approaches, the agencies of social control were primarily seen as reducing the magnitude of social problems or, at worst, as having no effect at all. By contrast, the labeling theorists believe that, inadvertently, public agencies designed to alleviate or reduce social problems have, in a very real sense, become part of the problem themselves, through their capacity to impose stigma of various sorts on the persons under their purview. Lemert noted that traditional sociology placed heavy reliance on the general idea that deviance leads to social control. But he later came to believe that the reverse—the idea that social control leads to deviance—was the "potentially richer premise."[29] In the more extreme statements of labeling theory, these agencies are seen as the main, or even the only, source of the very problems they supposedly combat.

Kai Erikson presents the perspective in this way: "Even the worst miscreant in society conforms most of the time, if only in the sense that he uses the correct silver at dinner, stops obediently at traffic lights, or in a hundred other ways respects the ordinary conventions of his group."[30] There are, therefore, two levels of analysis in the definitions of deviance: what is a

---

Critique, New York: Free Press, 1964. Clinard also presents an extensive review of studies employing the Mertonian typology.

29. Edwin M. Lemert, *Human Deviance, Social Problems, and Social Control*, Englewood Cliffs, N.J.: Prentice-Hall, 1967, p. 5.

30. Kai T. Erikson, *Wayward Puritans*, New York: Wiley, 1966, p. 6.

deviant act, and who is a deviant person? "When the community nominates someone to the deviant class, then, it is sifting a few *important* details out of the stream of behavior [the individual] has emitted and is in effect declaring that these details reflect the kind of person he 'really' is."[31] Erikson is referring to the idea of a "*master status*"—a single aspect of a person's set of roles (good husband, good father, Lion's Club member, bank robber, plumber) that completely overwhelms all other aspects. If a master status is bestowed by an official agency of government it confers a lasting stigma on the person.

Any agency with official power to impose a label on some individuals can bring about marked changes in their lives—not only through altering their experiences via prison or hospitalization, but by changing the impressions that important others have of them, their own self-image, and their chances for future employment. The labelers would argue that in many cases an agency takes marginal individuals who are not entirely committed to any position, closes off certain paths to them, and by various devices unintentionally forces them to accept its negative designation. By so doing, their deviant tendencies may well be heightened instead of reduced. The label (delinquent, psychotic) may become a sort of vicious self-fulfilling prophecy. The subjects may come to see themselves precisely as the agency sees them (e.g., "I am a dangerous criminal"), accept their label (with its own psychological rewards), and become that much more intractable. The emphasis in labeling theory is thus upon "*secondary deviation*"—the additional deviant behaviour that can be produced by society's reaction to an initial or "primary" deviation.[32]

The labeling approach as a coherent perspective can be traced back to Edwin Lemert in 1951, but it was Howard Becker who popularized the viewpoint in 1963 with a book entitled, appropriately, *Outsiders*.[33] Since then, numerous contributors have

---

31. *Ibid.*, p. 7, italics added.
32. Possibly the clearest case of vicious feedback is that of the homeless alcoholic. See P.J. Giffen, "The Revolving Door: A Functional Interpretation," *Canadian Review of Sociology and Anthropology*, 3, 1966, pp. 154-166.
33. Edwin M. Lemert, *Social Pathology*, New York: McGraw-Hill, 1951. (The book is definitely mistitled.) Howard S. Becker, *Outsiders: Studies in the Sociology of Deviance*, New York: Free Press, 1963.

advanced the perspective, including Aaron Cicourel, Albert Cohen, Kai Erikson, Erving Goffman, and Thomas Scheff. Labeling in contemporary sociology has had many of the qualities of a social movement; certain additional features and assumptions have made it the center of attention in current studies in social problems.[34] For instance, since few individuals are labeled out of the vast number who break the rules, it has been claimed that the enforcement of moral rules is essentially a political act. (That such is certainly true on occasion can be seen in detail in our chapter on the ideological basis of treatment.) And although not strictly required by the basic notion of labeling, it is also common for advocates to maintain that the defining of social problems is a political or at least ideological activity rather than one of community consensus. We have adopted this particular view throughout most of the book.

Critiques of labeling have come from several quarters. An early criticism by Gibbs emphasized the vagueness and lack of direction of the perspective.[35] Schur echoed this criticism, while finding great value in labeling's capacity for sensitizing the observer.[36] There has been a trend toward more systematic formulations of the approach,[37] as well as greater empirical scrutiny of its claims. Walter Gove has been especially active in this area.[38] Other major critics include Travis Hirschi, Edward

34. A good review of some of the earlier literature on the labeling perspective is found in John J. Hagan, "The Labelling Perspective, the Delinquent, and the Police: A Review of the Literature," *Canadian Journal of Corrections*, 14, 1972, pp. 150-165. For how labeling theory has developed in Canada see Robert A. Silverman and James J. Teevan, Jr., eds., *Crime in Canadian Society*, second edition, Toronto: Butterworths, 1980, pp. 148-150.

35. Jack P. Gibbs, "Conceptions of Deviant Behavior: The Old and the New," *Pacific Sociological Review*, 9, 1966, pp. 9-14.

36. Edwin M. Schur, "Reactions to Deviance: A Critical Assessment," *American Journal of Sociology*, 75, 1969, pp. 309-322.

37. For highly systematic presentations see Thomas Scheff, *Being Mentally Ill*, Chicago: Aldine, 1966, and Richard Hawkins and Gary Tiedeman, *The Creation of Deviance*, Columbus, Ohio: Merrill, 1975.

38. For instance, Walter R. Gove, "Societal Reaction as an Explanation of Mental Illness: An Evaluation," *American Sociological Review*, 35, 1970, pp. 873-884. For a review of the labeling perspective in terms of emotional problems, see M.S. Goldstein, "The Sociology of Mental Health and Illness," in *Annual Review of Sociology*, vol. 5, edited by Alex Inkeles et al., La Jolla, Cal.: Annual Reviews, 1979.

Sagarin, and Charles Tittle. Perhaps the two most thorough-going critiques have been prepared by Sagarin and Gove.[39] Gove and Scheff have engaged in one of the most vocal debates in recent sociology on the merits of labeling.

Reports of labeling's success or, conversely, its demise, are always greatly exaggerated, too simplistic, and premature.[40] The approach generates a great many specific hypotheses, some of which are confirmed while others are rejected. And yet still others turn out to have conflicting results, some of which support a labeling view while others do not.[41] Meanwhile, the *central core hypotheses* of the perspective are almost impossible to prove or disprove directly and conclusively, via a critical experiment, for both ethical and practical reasons.

Even the fiercest labeling advocate, furthermore, would concede that labeling does not always occur, that occasionally official intervention produces beneficial results. Conversely, even Tittle can concede that a labeling effect occasionally occurs.[42] The issue is therefore one of *degree*, which is always much harder to establish. Is the *principal effect* of official processing to (a) label, stigmatize, and hence channel negatively, (b) to provide help (psychiatric, or other rehabilitative) to those persons designated, or (c) is it to sanction offenders and hence, by their example, to deter others from the act and the same persons from doing it again (the deterrence argument)?[43]

39. Edward Sagarin, *Deviants and Deviance*, New York: Praeger, 1975, and *The Labelling of Deviance*, edited by Walter R. Gove, New York: Sage, 1975.
40. As one example Manning speaks of the "exhaustion" of labeling as a theory: Peter K. Manning, "On Deviance," *Contemporary Sociology*, 2, 1973, pp. 123-128.
41. Here are a few such examples. Some studies show that labeled youths have higher delinquency scores, (D.P. Farrington, "The Effects of Public Labelling," *British Journal of Criminology*, 17, 1977, pp. 112-126. See p. 114). Others indicate that this may not be the case (G. Fishman, "Can Labelling be Useful?" in *Youth Crime and Juvenile Justice*, edited by P.C. Friday and V.L. Stewart, New York: Praeger, 1977, p. 39.) See also, on the relevance of labeling to adolescent self-conceptions, Gary F. Jensen, "Labeling and Identity: Toward a Reconciliation of Divergent Findings," *Criminology*, 18, 1980, pp. 121-129.
42. See Gove, 1975, *op. cit.*, p. 175.
43. Tittle notes that the labeling perspective "completely overlooks the possibility that the threat of labelling may head off deviant careers by inhibiting deviance [through deterrence]." Charles R. Tittle, "Deterrents or Labeling?" *Social Forces*, 53, 1975, pp. 339-410. Quoted is p. 405.

Certainly (b) and (c) are the avowed intentions and purposes of the governmental agencies of social control, but is that in fact what usually happens or is (a) the more usual result?

Since occasional examples of each effect are not enough (the issue, to repeat, is the question of degree), and since critical experiments are ruled out, the debate thunders on, with much research—even much very clever research—but little conclusiveness. In a sense the two sides have been talking past each other, as Pretrunik, Feldman, and others have noted.[44] This will not satisfy critics such as Tittle, who staunchly demand empirical evidence.[45] As the newest of the major viewpoints, labeling is still in process of development and debate.

SUMMARY

Let us try to encapsule the principal features of each approach—doing major violence to the sense of the viewpoints, no doubt, by such brief descriptions.[46]
1. Social pathology sees social problems developing because of a "disorder" analogous to sickness in an organism. Weak or "defective" individuals must be weeded out for the organism to prosper. The more modern version sees aspects of the social system rather than specific individuals as the root cause of social problems.
2. The social disorganization approach focuses on norms, and sees social problems originating from various deficiencies in the

44. Petrunik feels that Gove's 1975 "demolition" of the labeling perspective, as not supported by the empirical evidence, was a case of first setting up a "sociological strawman" that did not really represent the views of the advocates and then destroying that strawman. See Michael Petrunik, "The Rise and Fall of 'Labelling Theory': The Construction and Destruction of a Sociological Strawman," Canadian Journal of Sociology, 5, 1980, pp. 213-235. Feldman at one point states that the differences between Scheff and Gove are nothing more than a case where "the same data are interpreted differently." Saul D. Feldman, Deciphering Deviance, Boston: Little, Brown, 1978, p. 310.
45. Tittle, op. cit.
46. The discussion in the present chapter has reviewed twentieth century approaches. For an excellent discussion of early (eighteenth and nineteenth century) theories of deviance see Lynn McDonald, The Sociology of Law and Order, Montreal: Book Centre, 1976.

cultural guidelines. There may be too few norms to cover all situations (normlessness, anomie), too many competing normative standards (culture conflict), or a lag in the transformation of some norms after other, related standards have changed (normative breakdown, cultural lag). All these perspectives were applied with great insight by the Chicago School to the social problems of the 1920's.

3. Conflict as the basis of social problems is in a way the simplest approach to comprehend. Social problems arise when self-conscious groups compete for scarce resources or for attainment of contradictory values. This approach becomes more involved when analysis is extended to less obvious situations in which the self-consciousness and/or cohesiveness of the groups is minimal. At this point, conflict theorists speak of an *inherent* conflict between groups with divergent self-interests.

4. Deviance theories arose to provide a social explanation for problematic actions by *individuals*. Deviant acts are seen as stemming from learning experiences, including vicarious learning of what has happened to others. It is aided by the learning of rationalizations ("techniques of neutralization" of conformist standards) and by deviant role models who can be admired. These aids, in turn, are seen as developing in deviant subcultures, which emerge in response to certain socially based strains shared by numerous individuals. The large amount of empirical work done under this perspective makes it the major point of departure today for contemporary theory—even for its critics.

5. Labeling theory is the most recent approach. It notes that most deviant acts are not observed and punished, and that most individuals who deviate are conformists in other respects and only marginally committed to their deviance. By the imposition of the majesty of the law in labeling some few persons as deviant, they are forced to surrender old roles and self-images, and to undergo unique experiences which, paradoxically from the standpoint of the intent of the labeler, may serve to heighten their deviant tendencies. Labeling thus focuses on the secondary deviation which may be brought about by society's reaction to the initial act.

Throughout the chapter we have adopted a roughly chronological standpoint, showing the various perspectives in the sequence in which they emerged into prominence. However it should not be supposed that newer approaches entirely superseded those that came before. Each new perspective has appeared brashly on the scene as the keystone to understanding, been criticized and then attacked by its successor, and ultimately humbled. But it is still true that each approach has left a residue of increased understanding of some aspects of social problems.

4 Defining Social Problems: The Victim, The Mass Media

The fact that certain circumstances are defined as problems raises several questions related to consensus and perception. The foremost are: Who defines a social problem? Who makes the diagnosis? The people involved? Outsiders? The people in charge, or, if you wish, the power structure? Those opposed to the power structure? At one time, for instance, there was no "French-Canadian problem" in Canada; at least, in the minds of most Canadians the condition was not so perceived.[1] Who finally made the official diagnosis? In that case it was primarily French-speaking Canadians themselves—a crucial feature of the present Canadian political situation, for "whoever initially identifies a social problem shapes the initial terms in which it will be debated,"[2] and this most important observation is reflected in the separatist orientation of the Parti Québécois. In addition to differences in initial labeling, dissensus may arise regarding the severity or urgency of a social problem and, in terms of policy making, on its national priority rating. Divergent opinions exist because, depending on where one is situated in society, what one's vested interests and experiences are, one will see phenomena somewhat differently.[3]

1. See Raymond Morris and C. Michael Lanphier, *Three Scales of Inequality: Perspectives on French-English Relations*, Toronto: Academic Press Canada, 1977.
2. James A. Jones, "Federal Efforts to Solve Contemporary Social Problems," in *Handbook on the Study of Social Problems*, edited by Erwin O. Smigel, Chicago: Rand McNally, 1971, p. 561.
3. We use the term "situated" globally to include sex, age, race, social class, as well as relevant psycho-social dimensions.

LIFE EXPERIENCES AND WORLD VIEW

This question of perception can be illustrated by the following example. After a dry period, farmers will welcome rain since they depend on it for their crops. City dwellers who intended to spend the weekend in the countryside are unhappy; their leisure plans are defeated. Motel owners and innkeepers will be disappointed because the expected flow of tourists will not materialize. Children with lenient parents may be happy because they can run in the rain and splash passers-by, but other children will be restrained at home and miserable. Therefore, one phenomenon, in this case rain, is perceived differently according to the situation of the individual and how one is affected by it. Life circumstances colour perceptions of even simple objects; this factor becomes much more complex and differentiated when it involves social situations.

It has been recently maintained, for instance, that heroin addiction came to be defined as a social problem by the population at large only when whites began to be affected by it. According to this perspective, when addiction was mainly restricted to black ghettos it was merely seen as a crime, or as deviance. It did not affect the population at large, and most whites were blissfully unconcerned about it—although social scientists and certain reformers had already sounded a warning. But when heroin addiction moved out of the ghettos, into the suburbs, into the schools and universities, not to mention the U.S. army, there was a general alarm. As numerous white adolescents became addicted, as white policemen arrested whites like themselves, and as numerous crimes were committed against whites in order to support an addiction, people came to be affected by this phenomenon in a different way. A vested interest in changing the situation developed. According to this perspective, heroin addiction came to be perceived as a social problem as a result of a shift in the circumstances of those who were in a position to define the situation. A similar process has also taken place with respect to venereal disease.

But it oversimplifies the role perception to maintain that vested or selfish interest is at the bottom of all divergent views on social problems. And to say that one's life experiences influence one's views about events that directly relate to those experiences is no great discovery. What is much more significant is the fact that differences in life experiences, repeated at length, can be equally effective in moulding impressions of social problems even where no personal interest is at stake and one has had no personal contact with a particular problem. We can see this most clearly in studies of the perceptual differences between persons in different occupations, since work consumes a major portion of the adult's waking existence. Even after intelligence and other variables are controlled for, remarkable differences in viewpoint between members of widely divergent occupations have been the rule. Even more striking are studies which show that, across several societies, members of similar occupational groups tend to stand in similar relation to other occupational groups in their society, in spite of considerable differences between the cultures studied. Manual workers, for instance, generally believe that human nature is more rigid than do non-manual workers of the same culture; they are more interested in job security, place greater stress on obedience in children, advocate greater economic readjustments, join fewer voluntary organizations, and manifest many other prominent similarities vis-a-vis non-manual occupations.[4] These findings are constant across cultures which are quite divergent in many respects, leading one to believe that the day-to-day experiences of people are of major importance in shaping their views of the world in general—a phenomenon studied under the rubric of the sociology of knowledge. Not surprisingly, this influence carries over into the definition of social problems by various groups in the population; in later chapters we will examine more closely just how their location in society influences the views of intellectuals (in Chapter 6) and judges (in Chapter 7).

But we have only begun to discuss the question initially raised, which was, "Who diagnoses a condition as a social problem?" We have only said so far that the definition of a social problem depends on the perception of those who take part in the

---

4. See, for example, Alex Inkeles, "Industrial Man: The Relation of Status to Experience, Perception, and Value," *American Journal of Sociology*, 66, 1961, pp. 1-31.

process of defining, and that, in turn, perceptions will be affected by the individuals' general situation in the society, by their situation vis-a-vis the phenomenon in question, and by their vested interests.[5] A corollary to be studied in this respect is the distinction between definition of a social problem by the individuals affected and definition by people who are, in their personal lives, relatively untouched by the problem. Definition by professional agents will be discussed in later chapters.

DEFINITIONS BY THOSE INVOLVED

People can be affected by a social problem along three general lines. The first is that of *voluntary involvement, with no immediately apparent victim other than the one person.* Here the persons afflicted by the problem—at least afflicted from the observer's point of view—are also the main agents or play the main voluntary roles in their affliction. Various mental disturbances, addiction, alcoholism, and such "victimless crimes" as prostitution[6] fall into this class. (It should be emphasized that this same group of individuals can be viewed under another perspective as victims of particular social conditions. In this interpretation their current affliction is the ultimate result of such conditions.)

The second category again concerns *voluntary involvement,* but covers activities in which the individuals who are the main actors in the problem do not suffer from their acts directly; they usually have *others as victims.* However, many criminals—the most ubiquitous actors in this category—eventually suffer because of their acts or the labels they receive. From this vantage point, society itself inflicts suffering—in the hope of reducing "aggregate suffering" by punishment of the few. From that point of view, criminals can be both willing agents and

5. For further discussion on the social origins of modes of thought, see the classic work on the sociology of knowledge, Karl Mannheim's, *Ideology and Utopia,* translated by Louis Wirth and Edward Shils, New York: Harvest, 1936.
6. We are using the concept of victimless crime for prostitution as it is referred to in the current literature. However, from other ideological positions, we can consider that prostitution has a victim in our society: the prostitute.

victims. Additionally, of course, criminals can be regarded as victims of social conditions which "drove" them to crime.

The third form of involvement consists of the victims of others' acts or society's failings, individuals who *suffer directly but accidentally* from a problem, playing only a derivative or even random role in their plight. Victims of theft, robbery, assault, or homicide come to mind first, but victims of discrimination, unemployment, as well as the children of divorce and of various types of psychologically broken homes fall into this category. Witnesses of violent crimes or other undesirable conditions may be included among victims, inasmuch as they are adversely affected by what took place.[7]

It could be advanced that since some crimes that are objectively inoffensive to the bystander and to the actor are defined as social problems by so many individuals, we should have a fourth category of individuals affected by a social problem: those whose values or sense of morality is offended.[8] This is a legitimate viewpoint; however, we have chosen to discuss such "victims" in the next chapter under the rubric of moral entrepreneurs. (Admittedly, most individuals whose values are threatened do not become active in moral crusades, but their viewpoint is nevertheless similar.)

Finally, it should be noted that individuals may be afflicted by a social problem in more than one way. This is not uncommon and indeed for some problems it is the rule. It is one of the pernicious aspects of heroin addiction, for instance, that individuals regularly progress from one status to the next. In the beginning, they are typically willing agents (possibly also victims of society's failings). As time passes they may first inflict unintentional suffering on their families, and then be driven to property crime to sustain their habit. Ultimately,

7. In some types of problem the suffering of each victim is minute but suffering is great for the aggregate, i.e., for society as a whole. Price fixing, for instance, may cost each customer only a few cents more, yet be quite costly for the economy. These and similar white-collar crimes typically do not evoke as much rage in the victim as in the expert who can see the overall damage.

8. Yet another affected category would be those people professionally involved in dealing with a perceived problem. We will consider these persons in Chapter 6.

many addicts become heroin peddlers themselves since this offers one of the more lucrative ways to earn the necessary money. At any point along this progression they may be incarcerated, and suffer both ritualistic (labeling) and practical miseries at the hands of the law. In this all too common career progression, an addict's classification may change from that of (1) willing participant to (2) aggressor to (3) victim.

A person's impression of whether a condition is a social problem, as well as its acknowledged degree of severity, will to a great extent depend on which of the three categories the definer falls into. (The definer may also be a relatively uninvolved observer—as discussed in subsequent chapters.) The victim, who is unwillingly affected and plays only an accidental role in, say, a theft, is likely to reach the conclusion that such a phenomenon is a major problem. He or she is directly involved but did not wish to be, probably having had no choice in a decision reached by another person.[9] The reactions of victims are varied but generally include feelings of unfairness, anger, hurt, and strong disapproval. This feeling will intensify as persons become aware of and establish contact with others who have gone through the same experience, a process known as "consciousness raising." Of considerable significance in terms of the strength of the reaction is the felt degree of intent—the degree to which the adverse condition is felt by the person to have been deliberate or intended by those responsible. This is why, for example, violent crime is viewed as a serious social problem by everyone whereas population pressure will be viewed as a major social problem only after careful study—even though it may in the long run prove a far more serious problem. So also, actions like price fixing, which hurt everyone a little bit, will be seen as less severe and accorded less attention than actions like muggings, which hurt a few people a great deal, even though the aggregate hurt may be much greater for the former.

---

9. The situation is not always so simple; as the new field of victimology teaches us, there may on occasion be recognizable patterns of victim-precipitated crime. See on the general subject, *Victimology: A New Focus*, vols. I and II, edited by I. Drapkin and E. Viano, Lexington, Mass.: Lexington Books, 1973.

A problematic situation will be perceived quite differently by the second category of actors, those who do not suffer immediately from their acts.[10] This is especially well illustrated in the case of organized crime. Some, who have been personally victimized, and their sympathizers, may call organized crime a social problem, but the actors themselves do everything to alter this definition and, especially, the consequences of the label—which can involve stiffer penalties, drainage of their illegal market, and loss of power and police cooperation. They frequently use their connections and advantages—legal and illegal—to silence opposition. For them, organized crime is first of all a means and a way of life, not a problem, and at times they publicly rationalize certain aspects of their role as providing a "public service." (Given a hypocrisy in Western cultures that frequently outlaws activities that many people enjoy doing, and plan to continue to do, they may on occasion be correct in this "public service" assessment.) If the actors have sufficient power and a certain popular legitimacy, a long time may elapse before the consequences of their acts are defined as problematic or, for that matter, are fully brought to the attention of the public.

The definition of a condition as problematic by those afflicted is typically most ambivalent in the first category, where the individuals are the main actors and also the sufferers. This ambivalence is partly created by the situational passivity of certain individuals (e.g., in mental disturbance) and, in other cases, because the afflicted enjoy aspects of their problem (e.g., heroin's effects) and, at least for the time being, are sufferers only in the minds of others. The individuals may or may not define their own situation as problematic. The nature of their reference group, awareness of alternatives, acquaintance with others in the same predicament—all are factors that contribute to their definition of their own situation.

The contention that only those persons who are directly afflicted by a situation have the right to label it as a problem is a difficult question to settle. For one thing, we would have to specify what is meant by "directly afflicted." For instance,

---

10. For a classical account of how delinquents rationalize their activities, see G.M. Sykes and D. Matza, "Techniques of Neutralization: A Theory of Delinquency," *American Sociological Review*, 22, 1957, pp. 664-670.

would we include those people whose moral values are threatened by the acts of others (people who disapprove of "free love," for instance)? And, if people with serious emotional disturbances never perceive their condition as deleterious, does it mean that mental disorders are not problematic? Does it consequently mean that nothing should be done to help these individuals, except to allow them to follow the threads of what are called their fantasies or withdrawals? The problem is a very complex one and the views on this topic cover a wide range. At one extreme are those who rigidly codify all behavioural peculiarities as at best neurotic, and insist on viewing any form of behaviour that is different from their norms as a symptom of an illness, which should be alleviated. At the other extreme are various groups who believe that only individuals can tell what is right and wrong for them and if they do not perceive their problems as such, then they are not problems. Within this conception, mental illness is considered to be only a myth, conceived by a repressive society that controls individual idiosyncrasies through a cohort of agents of social control (that is, the psychiatric community and its brethren).[11] Some advocates of this view also maintain that since it is the society which is mad, the individual's mental state, however it may appear to an observer, is a normal response to unhealthy stimuli. The person's conduct should therefore be left to run its course uninterrupted. Finally, psychological symptoms viewed as pathological by some are seen by others merely as "strategies to achieve autonomy and self-consistency."[12] "Normality" is merely a product of repression because it means conformity to an "abnormal society."[13]

Different types of treatment parallel these polar definitions of the nature of mental illness. At one extreme are shock and

11. See works referenced in Portland K. Frank, *The Anti-psychiatry Bibliography/Resource Guide*, Vancouver: Press Gang Publishers, 1979. Such positions led to the creation of the American Association for the Abolition of Involuntary Mental Hospitalization. A related ideological issue is raised by those who defined law enforcement officials as the source of social problems and the "criminals" they arrest as the victims. This is of course an extreme version of the labeling perspective (see Chapter 3).

12. See David Cooper, *The Death of the Family*, New York: Vintage Books, 1970.

13. R.D. Laing, *The Politics of Experience*, London: Penguin Books, 1967.

chemo-therapies, usually accompanied by a degree of social isolation. In the middle of the spectrum are various types of psychotherapies, and at the other extreme are found very liberal and radical therapies, some of which consist merely in allowing psychotic symptoms to be expressed within a protective and supportive environment but without chemical or psychiatric interference. However, all these viewpoints still share at least one result: the afflicted individual *is* treated differently, even if the differential treatment consists only in an overnight shelter for an "acting out."It is true that certain theoreticians in the field believe that each of us will sooner or later need to act out symptoms and that this is only a natural response to the pressures of an unhealthy environment. But, while it is the unhealthy environment that is the diagnosed ill in such views, a social problem is nevertheless perceived; moreover, it is at least implicitly held that those so touched need assistance, if only special understanding. Therefore, no matter what the philosophical orientation, a problem of some sort is definitely acknowledged. In the end it proves impossible to restrict the prerogative of defining a problem solely to those directly affected by it. But the notion that they should somehow have *greater* say in its delineation than others who are mere onlookers still seems reasonable. This last point will be examined again in the next chapter.

MASS MEDIA DEFINITIONS

The mass media have become exceedingly important as defining agents for social problems.[14] The reason, of course, is

14. Our discussion of the media centers on its definitional role. Mass communications can themselves be considered a social problem in certain contexts. The role of portrayals of violence and crime in the media, media's effect on audience passivity, instrusion into family relations, information pollution and overload—these are some of the issues evoked. See these and other questions examined in Joseph T. Klapper, *The Effects of Mass Communication*, Glencoe, Ill.: Free Press, 1959, part II; Orrin E. Klapp, *Currents of Unrest*, New York: Holt, Rinehart and Winston, 1972, Chapters 8 and 9; *Good, Bad, or Simply Inevitable? Selected Research Studies*, vol. 3 of Report of the Special Committee on Mass Media, Ottawa: Information Canada, 1970; *Roots of Aggression*, edited by Leonard Berkowitz, New York: Atherton, 1969; and

that the public in its definitional activity does not respond to reality but to its perception of that reality.[15] The media play a central role in shaping the image of reality that the public responds to: mass communication provides visibility for potential issues.[16] Professional and intellectual definers—discussed at length in Chapter 6—play their definitional role in great part through the media. The media also fulfill an important role in determining whether a problem is assigned legitimacy as a social issue or is discredited as illegitimate.[17]

In view of the nature of modern mass communications, a relatively small number of gate-keepers at the control centres can determine what we shall see and what we shall read.[18] There are many dangers inherent in this situation, in which what might be called a "delegate approach" to social problems has come into existence. This does not imply that the mass media are all-powerful in invoking a social problem label. Students of communication have long abandoned the simplistic viewpoint of a passive audience in favour of considering members of the audience as interpreters.[19] Rather it is the

---

Judith LaMarsh, *Report of Royal Commission on Violence in Media*, Toronto: Queen's Printer, 1977.

15. See, for general orientation, Peter L. Berger and Thomas Luckmann, *The Social Construction of Reality*, Garden City, N.Y.: Doubleday, 1966. For greater specificity with respect to mass media, see Daniel J. Boorstin, *Image: A Guide to Pseudo-Events in America*, New York: Atheneum, 1962.

16. Robert Ross and Graham L. Staines, "The Politics of Analyzing Social Problems," *Social Problems*, 20, 1972, p. 22.

17. *Ibid*. See also Ralph Turner, "The Public Perception of Protest," *American Sociological Review*, 34, 1969, pp. 815-831.

18. For an excellent illustration of the power of gate-keepers, see David Manning White, "The Gate-Keeper: A Study of the Selection of News," in *People, Society, and Mass Communication*, edited by Louis A. Dexter and David Manning White, New York: Free Press, 1968. The study superbly demonstrates the sheer impossibility of reporting all of the news that comes in via the wire services, let alone *all* news. Selectivity is unavoidable, and the power of the gate-keeper becomes unmistakable.

19. See the discussion in Franklin Fearing, "Human Communication," in Dexter and White, *ibid*. Certainly it is not impossible for a social problem to rise into prominence with very little help from the media. The environmentalist movement, for example, seems to have come to the attention of the daily press very belatedly. See A. Clay Schoenfeld *et al.*, "Constructing a Social Problem: The Press and the Environment," *Social Problems*, 27, 1979, pp. 38-61.

negative side, that *abstention* by the media can *preclude* recognition of a problem, which is so important. In this respect the importance of the "gate-keepers" in mass communication can hardly be overemphasized. This possibility, the potential to bring some issues to the fore and relegate others to obscurity, is known as *agenda setting*. Who the persons are at the key decision-making posts in television, newspapers, and other media—their personal backgrounds and social position—has come under increasing scrutiny in recent years.[20] There has been increasing concentration of ownership of the media into a few hands, such as newspaper chain concentration, or communities in which all media (radio, newspaper, etc.) are controlled by a single owner. With the power this conveys for informal censorship, these trends have interested American congressional investigating committees and a Canadian royal commission of inquiry.[21]

A prime danger inherent in the mass media definition of social problems is that it may invite only the briefest and most superficial public commitment to solving a problem. Because of the nature of commercialized mass culture, social problems tend to become fads when portrayed by the media. They are "sold" to the public, packaged in attractive, sensationalist wrappings. Newspaper reports of crime waves, for example, are as old as newspapers themselves, and bear only the vaguest relationship to actual fluctuations in number of offenses.[22] Because the mass media are money-making ventures, if one

20. See Herbert Gans, *Deciding What's News*, New York: Pantheon Books, 1979. Canadians have become very sensitive to foreign controls and inputs. See Benjamin D. Singer, "American Invasion of the Mass Media in Canada," in *Critical Issues in Canadian Society*, edited by Craig L. Boydell *et al.*, Toronto: Holt, Rinehart and Winston of Canada, 1971, pp. 423-436.
21. For discussions of concentration in the Canadian media see Chapter 3 in Paul Rutherford, *The Making of the Canadian Media*, Toronto: McGraw-Hill Ryerson, 1978; Dick MacDonald, "Communication: The State of the Canadian News Media," pp. 131-140 in Gertrude Joch *et al.*, *Studies in Canadian Communications*, Montreal: McGill University Printing Service, 1975. Findings of the recent Kent royal commission have been widely discussed in newspaper articles.
22. For an excellent example of how crime waves are constructed in the media, see Mark Fishman, "Crime Waves as Ideology," *Social Problems*, 25, 1978, pp. 531-543.

topic becomes obsolete by no longer attracting as many viewers or readers, it is reasonable to expect a shift to another, more lucrative fad. Even the news reports are affected by the need for novelty. When a problem bursts into public consciousness, it may make the news broadcasts every evening for an entire month, or even longer, as for instance was the case with the hostage crisis in Iran. But rarely is such attention sustained; normally after a few weeks it is no longer news: it is a fact. The mass media neglect it and so do we. It has lost its topicality. One could get the impression that the situation is much improved, or even resolved. We have perhaps become conditioned to having others think for us and define situations for us via the media. When the media shift gear, we tend to erase from our consciousness what no longer appears on the screen. We may even be foolish enough to believe that the problem has vanished, just because we no longer see it. Our conceptions of social problems themselves become fads, temporarily gripping and soon to drift into oblivion—but not erased from reality.[23]

What is it that makes something "newsworthy," at least in the mind of the gate-keeper? We have already touched on the gate-keeper aspect itself, and on the presumed need for topicality or frequent change of topic. One additional feature is the notion of the necessary rhythm or speed of the event before it becomes news. Every occurrence has a time-span needed for the event to unfold itself; the less the speed at which an event unfolds matches the usual frequency or speed of events reported by a communications medium, the less likely it will be communicated as news by that medium. News media in general concentrate on relatively fast-breaking events. The slow, glacial emergence of some problems does not lend itself to news

23. One could easily adopt McLuhan's statement that newspaper editors have discovered that "news is what gets printed. If it isn't in print, it isn't news." He might have said, "if it isn't in print, it isn't a social problem." Marshall McLuhan, "The Electronic Age—The Age of Implosion," in *Mass Media in Canada*, by John A. Irvin, Toronto: Ryerson Press, 1962, pp. 179-205. One other effect of this is to bias the impact of news according to its *availability*. Thus the Vietnam War was directly accessible to Western news media, and appeared on television screens daily for years in gory detail, generating unprecedented emotional protest. In contrast, the similar war in Afganistan receives very little coverage, because Western news personnel are forbidden entry, and therefore has little impact and generates only scattered protest.

presentation, and although these problems may eventually become of overwhelming importance they are rarely reported. The population explosion is an excellent case in point. Here we have an event which is shaping the destiny of nations and affecting the quality of life of every inhabitant of the planet, yet it is not news. At least, it is not news as ordinarily considered. It is too slow in its progress. On no single day does the population explosion leap out in some fashion, like the death of a famous movie star. So too the gradual despoliation of lakes from acid rain, or the gradual erosion of topsoil, or the gradual deforestation of the globe, do not generate news on any given day, and are "lost." If, however, one hundred persons splash green paint on a monument in protest against deforestation, that will make the news.[24] The long-run effect of such a strange situation is clearly to grossly distort public understanding of major forces at work in the world, with a commensurate misunderstanding of social problems.

The hypothetical green-paint demonstration mentioned above brings us to a related topic: *the manufacture of news*. The notion of manufacturing can be considered in two (related) ways. The broader aspects have to do with the growing recognition that life is not a set of discrete public events that can simply be mirrored by newspeople. News is manufactured; it is a product—a product not only of reality-describing activities but of reality-making activities. Hence a critical sociological task, reflected in a growing list of studies, is to examine concretely newsworkers' transformations of the everyday world into published or broadcast stories.[25] The other (related) meaning of "manufactured" refers to news that is deliberately created solely in order to convey a particular message. Daniel Boorstin's book, *Image*, deals extensively with media events that have no independent reason for existence other than to attract media attention and get a particular message across.

24. For more on the topic of this paragraph see Johan Galtung and Mari Ruge, "Structuring and Selecting News," in *The Manufacture of News*, edited by S. Cohen and J. Young, Beverly Hills: Sage, 1973.
25. As exemplars of the trend see Cohen and Young, *ibid*; Mark Fishman, *Manufacturing the News*, Austin: University of Texas Press, 1980; Gaye Tuchman, *Making News: A Study in the Construction of Reality*, New York: Free Press, 1978.

Such "happenings" are engineered or staged. Public demonstrations, hunger strikes, and similar events are sufficiently striking and unusual to be newsworthy; they are the little people's equivalent of the press conference of the powerful— also a pure media event.

Related to the idea of the manufacturing of news is the powerful new conception of *bureaucratic propaganda*. Propaganda was formerly considered a tool of national governments, akin to psychological warfare,[26] or possibly to religious proselytization (where the term propaganda originated). But recently an extension of the term has been proposed, in order to include corporations, industries, and government bureaucracies.[27] Bureaucratic propaganda encompasses vast efforts we have all noticed at one time or another to bring an audience around to the special viewpoint of a particular bureaucracy. It includes such important activities as *institutional advertising*, in which, for instance, oil companies attempt to build trust or to show that their profits were justified, rather than just to sell x brand of gasoline. It includes as well all manner of puffery by government agencies on what a great job they did (hundreds of thousands of cases processed), or conversely, what a terrible task they are facing (rising crime in the streets). In bureaucratic propaganda, the power of major institutions in modern society is harnessed to manipulate or at least shift the attention of the media in the desired direction.

Most social problems are not concerns of the majority of citizens, so the role of important elites and the media in disseminating ideas and "facts" is frequently crucial in influencing public opinion. Inasmuch as the public relies on the media for information, the magnitude of a problem may be misinterpreted. For instance, a survey carried out in Colorado indicated that perception of the danger from certain crimes was related to the coverage they received in the newspapers rather than to the crime rates themselves. Lynn McDonald has provided overwhelming evidence of the poor fit between fluctuat-

---

26. See Terence H. Qualter, *Propaganda and Psychological Warfare*, New York: Random House, 1962.
27. See the innovative work by David L. Altheide and John M. Johnson, *Bureaucratic Propaganda*, Boston: Allyn and Bacon, 1980.

ing fears of crime and actual shifts in the volume of crime in the Canadian context.[28] Media emphasis on certain problems blinds us to others still only vaguely perceived, a situation which may have serious consequences. For instance, some black leaders have attacked the emphasis on pollution as a false issue which diverts attention away from the "truly severe crises" in the cities. The treatment of crime has been subjected to similar criticism. Burglaries attract far greater press coverage than white-collar crimes or governmentally sanctioned political crimes, although the latter may cost citizens millions of times the losses sufferd from the former, or even weaken important political freedoms.[29] Popular emphasis or new problems—or more sensational ones—may relegate others already diagnosed to the background, or even lead to an inadvertent blackout of coverage.[30] The emphasis on drug addiction in Canada can be mentioned here in contrast to what is said to be the country's far greater problem—alcoholism.[31] We have Gallup Polls, running from 1935 through the late 1970's, showing certain patterns in public definitions of problems, and identifying the kind of concerns held by the public at different times.[32] As Liazos points

28. F. James Davis, "Crime News in Colorado Newspapers," *American Journal of Sociology*, 57, 1952, pp. 325-330. Lynn McDonald, *The Sociology of Law and Order*, Montreal: Book Centre, 1976. See also Inez Dussuyer, *Crime News: A Study of 40 Ontario Newspapers*, Toronto: University of Toronto Centre of Criminology, 1979. Lack of knowledge and systematic misunderstandings about crime are endemic. See *Perception in Criminology*, edited by R.L. Henshel and R. Silverman, New York: Columbia University Press, 1975.

29. See August Bequai, *White-Collar Crime: A 20th Century Crisis*, Lexington, Mass.: Lexington Books, 1978; Nelson Blackstock, *COINTELPRO: The FBI's Secret War on Political Freedom*, New York: Random House, 1975; Julian Roebuck and Stanley C. Weeber, *Political Crime in the United States: Analyzing Crime By and Against Government*, New York: Praeger, 1978.

30. See Chapter 2 of James C. Hackler, *The Prevention of Youthful Crime: The Great Stumble Forward*, Toronto: Methuen, 1978.

31. See *Cannabis* (LeDain Report), Report of the Commission of Inquiry into the Non-Medical Use of Drugs, Ottawa: Information Canada, 1972. This report even remarks (p. 267) that drug addiction in Canada has never reached social problem stage. The contrast with alcohol is pointed out. Ontario alone has some 100,000 alcoholics, and there are an estimated 670,000 throughout Canada. See C. Hanley, *Mental Health in Ontario*, A Study for the Committee on the Healing Arts, Toronto: Queen's Printer, 1970; *The Toronto Star*, December 18, 1972, p. 1.

32. See these polls surveyed in Robert H. Lauer, "Defining Social Problems: Public and Professional Perspectives," *Social Problems*, 22, 1976, pp. 122-128.

out, however, the responses thus obtained turn out to be largely dictated by the current fads of the media, which in turn are greatly affected by centres of power.[33]

SUMMARY

In this chapter we have broached the central question of social problems: why some conditions become so defined, why others do not, why some are seen as more serious problems than others, or why some conditions exist for very long periods before being labeled problematic. Laying the groundwork for discussions in subsequent chapters, these questions were initially examined from the standpoint of the sociology of knowledge—the influence of life experiences and one's social location on views about the world, including aspects remote from one's own existence.

The discussion then covered two possible sources of social problem views. First, the standpoint of the person directly involved was examined through the eyes of the victim of the problem, and from the point of view of the willing participant (bringing up the issues of victimless crime, the marginal status of much organized crime, and persons who do not feel they have a psychiatric problem that someone else feels they have). Second, the singular importance of the mass media of communication in shaping public views and policies toward social problems was emphasized. The numerous distortions that can arise from concentration of ownership and from gate-keeper editorial control were stressed, as were the distorting requirements of topicality and event "velocity." The agenda-setting potential of the media was illustrated by reference to a percep-

---

A Canadian survey is reported in Reginald W. Bibby, "Consensus in Diversity: An Examination of Canadian Social Problem Perception," *International Journal of Comparative Sociology*, 20, 1979, pp. 274-282. For relevant findings on the international scale see Graeme Newman, *Comparative Deviance: Perception and Law in Six Cultures*, New York: Elsevier, 1976.

33. Alexander Liazos, "The Poverty of the Sociology of Deviance: Nuts, Sluts, and Perverts," *Social Problems*, 20, 1972, pp. 103-120.

tion of "crime waves" that bore no relationship to actual changes in volume of crime. Finally, the ability of bureaucratic propaganda to manufacture news was stressed. The next two chapters pursue our basic question, focusing on the definitional activities of moral entrepreneurs, intellectuals, and experts.

5 Defining Social Problems: Moral Entrepreneurship

In the previous chapter we discussed two major sources of definition for social problems: people who are afflicted by them, be it directly or indirectly, and the mass media. A third category consists of *moral entrepreneurs*, groups or individuals who develop legislation protecting what they see as threatened morality. With this group, we begin our discussion of ideology (and vested interest) as a basis for definition and for treatment, a topic that will be further developed in subsequent chapters.[1]

CRIME AND THE ORIGINS OF CRIMINAL LAWS

Crime is generally considered one of the most severe of social problems, and since it also provides us with the sharpest definitions of what constitute specific cases of the problem, it is an excellent place to begin our discussion. What constitutes a social problem here? Obviously, a specific case of crime. But what *is* crime, generally speaking? One searches through various possibilities (crime as sin, crime as wickedness) but one invariably arrives at what have been called the *legal interpretation* and the *social interpretation* (or the legal and social definitions) of crime.[2] These definitions stand in competition with one another, each having special advantages.

The legal interpretation of crime is quite simple: crime is whatever appears on the statutes at a particular time and

1. See Karl Mannheim, *Ideology and Utopia*, translated by Louis Wirth and Edward Shils, New York: Harvest Book, 1936.
2. See Elmer H. Johnson, *Crime, Correction and Society*, revised edition, Homewood, Ill.: Dorsey Press, 1968, pp. 13-15. A good discussion is contained in Robert A. Silverman and James J. Teevan, Jr., eds., *Crime in Canadian Society*, second edition, Toronto: Butterworths, 1980, pp. 3-5.

place—it is whatever the law says it is. This has the advantage of simplicity, and it is also relatively precise.[3] But it lacks any logical or theoretical cohesion. The social interpretation, on the other hand, is relatively sophisticated theoretically but lacking in precision. According to the social perspective, a crime is a contranormative act which is regarded as so unpleasant by the community that it reserves its severest sanctions for such actions. This interpretation assumes that there will be high agreement among community members about the severity of acts, yet this assumption of consensus is not borne out in fact.[4] The totally different attitudes of conservatives and liberals on the relative harm of pollution and drug use might be illustrative of the difficulties involved in the social interpretation. Even for those crimes in which there does appear to be a consensus on a hierarchy of severity, the hierarchy found, in surveys, to be held by the public does not always correspond to the severity of official sanctions.[5] What is more, some extremely contranormative acts such as cannibalism are not found in the statutes as distinct offenses.

Yet, for all of its weaknesses, the social interpretation at least provides a certain theoretical unity for acts classified as criminal. In contrast, although the legal interpretation is more precise, it amounts to the idea that *crime is whatever legislators say it is*.[6] We thus find absurd crimes on record. In Louisiana a theatre manager is guilty of a misdemeanour if he allows people to be seated after a performance has started. In the state of Arkansas, one may not erect a lunch counter on Decoration Day within a half-mile of a Confederate cemetery. The City Council of Moose Jaw, Saskatchewan, passed a bylaw in 1971 making walking on the left side of sidewalks illegal and punishable by a

3. There is still considerable latitude for discretion and for abuse, as we note in the chapter on differential treatment.
4. See the analysis of various sectors of the population in Craig L. Boydell and Carl F. Grindstaff, "Public Attitudes Toward Legal Sanctions for Drug and Abortion Offenses," *Canadian Journal of Criminology and Corrections*, 13, 1971, pp. 209-232.
5. See the Sellin-Wolfgang scale of severity of offenses, in Thorstein Sellin and Marvin Wolfgang, *The Measurement of Delinquency*, New York: Wiley, 1964.
6. Furthermore the insistence on legal precision can itself result in absurd arbitrariness. See illustration of this point in James C. Hackler, *The Prevention of Youthful Crime: The Great Stumble Forward*, Toronto: Methuen, 1978, p. 5.

$100 fine or thirty days in jail, maximum sentence. Numerous other absurd examples could be provided.

Technically, anyone who does these things performs a criminal act, just as if he had murdered his wife, sold heroin, incited others to riot, embezzled funds, falsified his income tax, vandalized a school building, or lied under oath. The only thing the above elements have in common, outside of their illegal character, is that someone did not like them. Obviously, if *no one* liked them they would not be illegal—viz. cannibalism, which is rarely included in the criminal law. Clearly some people do like to embezzle funds or damage school buildings. Why should their judgment not be taken instead of someone else's?

Unfortunately for those who assume a perfect match between the legal and social interpretations, this match does not exist. There are too many illegal acts which no one regards as "bad" and too many "bad" acts which are not criminal. If some unscrupulous people get a little old lady in a wheelchair to sign over all of her savings for something of very low value, and then brag about it, they are looked down upon but this is not illegal. Examples abound of the lack of fit between the two definitions of crime.[7]

It should be obvious from the above discussion why, if we utilize the legal interpretation, we have no adequate theory (or even theories) of the causes of criminal behaviour. Criminal acts under this perspective have neither logical nor psycho-social unity. We can, of course, have theories about the causes of *specific* crimes, just as for any other form of human behaviour. But crime *as it appears in the statutes is not a meaningful collection of actions from a social or psychological standpoint.* As Quinney notes, "crime is not inherent in behavior, but is a judgment made by some about the actions and characteristics of others."[8]

---

7. Many excellent examples of this point are given in Chapter 2 of Edmund Vaz, *Aspects of Deviance*, Toronto: Prentice-Hall of Canada, 1976. As will be discussed, the very action of making something illegal can by itself make the deed seem nasty or dirty to many people. So the fact that there is a certain degree of "fit" between the two interpretations should not be surprising.

8. Richard Quinney, *The Social Reality of Crime*, Boston: Little, Brown, 1970, p. 16. Unfortunately, because of factors of cost and manpower, social research

Since persons are prosecuted under the legal interpretation (that is, under the criminal code), it is worthwhile to determine precisely how criminal interpretations come into being. Just who decides what should be against the law? The answer varies, of course, in different societies and at different times, but one clear conclusion to be reached is that laws are universally made by a very limited number of persons, although they subsequently become binding for others. In Western democratic societies the criminal law is formulated by representatives in legislatures.[9]

Under democratic theory such persons represent the wishes of their constitutents with respect to the laws they promulgate. Without being overly critical of the representative principle, it nevertheless must be noted that, with respect to criminal law, the legislators cannot avoid—virtually by definition—favouring some of their constituents over others. What guides them in their decisions on which persons to listen to?

In some cases the legislative decision is easy. Murder has been an offense as long as law has been recorded, and it is almost meaningless to speak of a decision to discriminate against the murderer, or that murderers deserve the same consideration as a group with legitimate interests.[10] Many people think of all criminal law in this fashion, while in reality criminal law in most cases does involve a discrimination against what some persons regard as legitimate activities. It has been noted that a "law explosion" has taken place in North America in the twentieth century, in terms of the rapidity with which formerly legal acts have been criminalized. Americans in particular are frequently noted by observers to have an excessive faith in the efficacy of the law to solve social problems. We will reconsider some aspects of this extensive criminalization

---

is often required to use official statistics collected under less meaningful social categories. This is frequently the case in the study of crime.

9. For brevity we exclude "judge-made law," that is, judicial decisions which have the effect of radically altering statutory law. See Chapter 7 on differential treatment for a related discussion.

10. It is not, however, so meaningless to speak of decisions on such matters as justifiable homicide.

momentarily, but at this juncture the point is that each of these additional laws has been added at the expense of certain persons or interests and for the benefit of others. The obviousness of such traditionally forbidden acts as murder and robbery does not necessarily extend to the birth of these new prohibitions.

What answers there are can be derived from an examination of two aspects of the law-making process: the backgrounds of the legislators themselves and the types of advice they receive from what have been pejoratively called "moral entrepreneurs" and positively termed "social reformers." Legislators in various countries tend to be non-representative of the population in terms of social class and occupation, however much they may be representative in other respects. In the Soviet Union, engineers are in the majority in decision-making bodies; in China, one's family background must be free of bourgeois affiliations. In North America, lawyers are vastly over-represented in legislative bodies, and in virtually all Western, industrialized societies, the upper middle class and upper class form the bulk of the elected leadership. In all cases the vast majority of legislators are males rather than females, and old rather than young. These characteristics enter into the nature of the laws passed by such persons not only because of the vested interests possible in these circumstances, although there are transparent instances of such, but also because the common backgrounds of the legislators means that they share certain life experiences and outlooks. It may also mean that, as a body, they are blind to certain experiences and correspondingly cannot appreciate certain points of view.[11] This similarity of background is one ingredient in understanding the types of criminal legislation that are passed, and the types of persons and acts deemed to be "outside the pale" of decency.

MORAL ENTREPRENEURS

Moral entrepreneurs were defined at the outset of this chapter

11. See Gwynn Nettler's perceptive article, "Good Men, Bad Men, and the Perception of Reality," *Sociometry*, 24, 1961, pp. 279-294.

as groups and individuals who develop or advocate legislation protecting what they see as threatened morality. In effect they try to legislate morality, and contrary to conventional wisdom they sometimes succeed. Moral entrepreneurs are found today demanding, in various places, anti-pornography legislation, laws to control gambling or prostitution, or mandatory religious prayers in the schools. In earlier periods they have tried to control the teaching of evolution—a drive that has recently reappeared via the efforts of the Moral Majority organization in the United States. In the most famous instance, moral entrepreneurs succeeded for a time in prohibiting the sale of intoxicating beverages in the United States. Prohibition is a fine example not only of moral enterprising but also of the lack of public consensus regarding many laws for which there are criminal penalties.[12]

The term moral entrepreneur was created by Howard Becker in what has become a classic study of the development of anti-marijuana legislation.[13] In his view of this development, Becker found that no marijuana users were consulted (although it was not illegal in many states to use marijuana at that time), that claims of dire effects from the substance were accepted without expert testimony, and that the driving force behind the legislation was federal narcotics agents who wished to expand the scope of their operations.[14] Quinney presents an equally cogent analysis of "blue law" (Sunday closing) legislation in terms of business interests which could be hurt by competition on Sunday, and which suddenly became intensely interested in morality.[15]

12. Resistance to prohibition was strongest in the large cities of the United States. At that time, due to unequal districting, American legislatures were dominated by representatives of rural areas.
13. Howard S. Becker, "The Marijuana Tax Act," in *Outsiders: Studies in the Sociology of Deviance*, by Howard S. Becker, New York: Free Press, 1963.
14. For accounts of similar developments in Canada, tracing Canadian narcotics legislation to conflict between Chinese immigrants and dominant English-speaking culture, see Shirley J. Cook, "Canadian Narcotics Legislation, 1908-1923: A Conflict Model Interpretation," *Canadian Review of Sociology and Anthropology*, 6, 1969, pp. 36-46; Robert Solomon and T. Madison, "The Evolution of Non-Medical Opiate Use in Canada, 1870-1929," *Drug Forum*, 5, 1977, pp. 239-249.
15. Quinney, *op. cit.*, pp. 65-70.

The feasibility of moral entrepreneurship in legislating morality is aided by a curious circular process in which what is made against the law becomes immoral *by this fact* for many people. Although the introduction of legislation can have a backlash—as happened with prohibition and seems to be occurring today with marijuana—more frequently morality legislation not only alters actions but even the attitudes of persons toward the deed.[16]

The law explosion referred to earlier has several dimensions, including an increase in civil adjudication which is not of particular interest here. One of its most striking aspects is a broad expansion of criminal legislation beyond what might be considered the traditional business of the criminal code. In part this has been mandated by the increasing complexity and interdependence of modern society, and by expansion of the law to include such humanitarian additions as food and drug laws. In large part, however, an increasingly burdensome aspect of the criminal law has been what some refer to as *crimes without victims*—the use of the criminal sanction to forbid acts in which no one is injured. These crimes include many of the most controversial—and unenforceable—laws.[17] Actions in which the only individual concerned is happy with his/her act, or in which the several persons concerned are all satisfied, are difficult to justify as crimes merely because someone else who *thinks* about the acts does not like them. Such conditions apply to most criminal cases involving pornography, prostitution, homosexuality, and numerous other prohibited or restricted activities. A rising tide of opinion has challenged the conventional legal wisdom on these matters, and victimless crime thus

16. See Walker and Argyle for a somewhat different view. Nigel Walker and Michael Argyle, "Does the Law Affect Moral Judgments?" *British Journal of Criminology*, 4, 1964, pp. 570-581. An intriguing companion notion is the finding that laws that are on the books but never strongly enforced despite blatant, well-known violations gradually become *re-legitimized* in the public's attitudes. See A.E. McCormick, Jr., "Rule Enforcement and Moral Indignation," *Social Problems*, 25, 1977, pp. 30-39.
17. See Herbert L. Packer, *The Limits of the Criminal Sanction*, Stanford, Calif.: Stanford University Press, 1968; Edwin Schur, *Crimes Without Victims*, Englewood Cliffs, N.J.: Prentice-Hall, 1965; Sanford H. Kadish, "The Crisis of Over-criminalization," *The Annals*, 374, 1967, pp. 157-170; Gilbert Geis, *Not the Law's Business*, New York: Schocken Books, 1979.

provides an excellent illustration of the power dimension in legislation.[18]

Paralleling the notion of victimless crimes is the older distinction in legal philosophy between crimes that are *mala in se* and other crimes that are *mala prohibita*. Very roughly, this can be translated as crimes that are bad in themselves and crimes that are bad because prohibited. Crimes *mala in se* are what one ordinarily thinks of when considering crime: offenses such as homicide or rape. Even if a jurisdiction somewhere were to legalize such activities, virtually all cultures regard them as bad or evil in themselves. By contrast, crimes *mala prohibita* include offenses created for bureaucratic convenience, such as failure to file income tax returns by a given date, or offenses disruptive of order, such as driving down the wrong side of the street.[19] One reason that the distinction is valuable is that it helps us to recognize that the law explosion has consisted in large part of a vast expansion of crimes *mala prohibita*. The essential question about which there is continued debate is whether or not victimless crimes are merely crimes *mala prohibita*.[20]

THE ROLE OF RELIGION

Thus far we have concentrated on the power to decide what the *criminal* component of social problems should be; however, the power to mediate the critical definition is equally important in other areas. In many societies, religion has a power of definition approaching that of legislation. The relative power of religion and state in this crucial arena is an interesting issue, one which oscillates interminably. After the Mexican Revolution of 1911,

18. De-criminalization has made major inroads in the past decade in northern Europe and Canada (for example, Canada's Omnibus Bill legalized homosexual acts under specified conditions). In the United States, penalties for marijuana possession have been reduced in several states, but it is safe to say that de-criminalization is relatively weak in North America.
19. For some good examples of the distinction see Chapter 2 of Vaz, *op. cit.*, especially pp. 21-22.
20. For an excellent exposition of the issues of *mala in se* versus *prohibita*, social versus legal interpretations of crime, and of victimless crime, see Edward Sagarin, *Deviants and Deviance*, New York: Praeger, 1975.

for instance, since the Catholic Church had supported the old regime, clerics were shorn of much of their power. More recently, however, they have gradually regained much of their lost potency. The states of Israel and Iran—differing in so many other respects—are both avowedly religiously based, on Judaism and Islam respectively, and experience constant intrusion of religious principles and definitions into secular affairs. In such situations, religion and state interpenetrate in terms of defining social problems and forbidding certain activities by means of the criminal law. During the Middle Ages in Europe the Church was in fact the State in most senses of the word, with its own ecclesiastical courts, its own law, prisons, and its own taxes. Even in apparently secular states, for those with a single dominant religion (e.g., Italy, the Irish Republic) the interpenetration can be quite powerful, e.g., in divorce legislation.[21] On the other hand, in Poland, an officially atheist country, the Catholic Church wields immense power in secular affairs, but does so outside of the official criminal law which is controlled by the Communist Party. A comparative, cross-cultural study of such matters, apart from the hints of complexity just given, is beyond the scope of this book, and we will henceforth concentrate on the situation closer to home.[22]

In our own society, the papal encyclical on birth control, the traditional opposition of the Catholic Church to divorce, and general clerical resistance to legal abortion has meant—from the sociologist's standpoint—the persistence of unmanaged problems of unhappy couples and unwanted (and sometimes battered) children. And although overpopulation is not a problem in Canada itself, whenever global concerns are addressed it becomes a critical social problem. From a clerical

21. The history of the intrusion of English Protestantism into Catholic Ireland, taking effect only in the north (Ulster), is itself a striking display of church combining with the power of state. It reminds us that England at one time had an official religion, as did most European countries. See Desmond Bowen, *The Protestant Crusade in Ireland, 1800-1870*, Montreal: McGill-Queens University Press, 1978.
22. For studies from several cultures on the nature of the linkage between the criminal law and popular views about deviance (not necessarily religious-based views), see Graeme Newman, *Comparative Deviance: Perception and Law in Six Cultures*, New York: Elsevier, 1976.

point of view it is exactly the opposite: divorce, contraception, and abortion have been seen as the critical problems. Insofar as these have been staved off, "moral problems" have been averted; insofar as they have been allowed, society has regressed morally. This is not to say that all Catholics, or even all clerics, agree with such positions, nor that such social problems as over-population, unhappy homes, or unwanted children are unrecognized by the religious sector. Indeed there are Catholic sociologists and clerics who work vigorously towards the amelioration of these problems. Rather, a claim is made based on religious belief that there is a right way (e.g., the rhythm method) and a wrong way (e.g., abortion, divorce) to handle these problems, so that if the wrong way is used it becomes a problem in itself.

Although particular evaluations originate in the religious sector, they often come to be accepted by other problem-solving agencies in the community. In this way the increasing frequency of divorce is widely conceptualized as a social problem, not only by religious persons to whom it is intolerable, but also by non-religious persons, and ultimately by welfare agencies. In societies in which a single religion is pre-eminent, the alliance of Church and State (even if unofficial) results in an inability to enact certain types of ameliorative legislation. Even in societies with several religions, the alliance of state and religion is seen in the frequent recourse to legislation to deal with religiously defined social problems. The Prohibition Movement represented the high point of religious definitional power in the United States; its resounding failure may have had much to do with the rise of competing definitional powers which we will discuss in a moment. But religion's labeling power is still very much alive, if severely weakened. Contemporary activities are considerably more circumspect. The tendency today is to downplay the seriousness of social problems where recognition seems likely to call for morally undesirable remedies. In this way for many years the Catholic Church minimized the severity of population problems.[23]

23. See, e.g., Monsignor George A. Kelly, *Overpopulation: A Catholic View*, New York: Paulist Press, 1960.

In some societies the religious establishment is still an extremely powerful factor in the definition of social problems and the acceptability of means of resolution. Obviously this was even more the case in the past and, once a social phenomenon had been defined as a problem, the label tended to *persist* as though by inertia. Many of the labels of today are accurately described as holdovers from an era of powerful religious movements. Although the role of religion in the definitional process is far from over, as we are reminded by recurrent campaigns against various forms of "indecency," its place in Western societies has become increasingly usurped by two relatively recent perspectives—what we might call the *egalitarian* and *psychiatric perspectives*. These are the expansionist perspectives of the day: despite periodic fluctuations, the long-term historical trend of religious influence is downward. While religious definitions retreat (or at best hold their own), new conceptions of social problems arise to take their place, based either on perceived inequalities in the structuring of rewards and opportunities in society (the egalitarian perspective) or on real or imagined mental difficulties (the psychiatric perspective).[24]

It should not be supposed that organized religion has been concerned solely with the preservation of conventional morality; links between egalitarian social movements and conventional religion have sometimes been very close. The closeness or remoteness has varied from issue to issue. The earliest egalitarian movements in the modern era, those toward legal equality before the law and the abolition of an hereditary aristocracy (American and French Revolutions) were products of the Age of Reason (see Chapter 2) and derived very little impetus from religious forces.[25] On the other hand, the anti-

24. Since psychiatric definitions are typically seen as medical and scientific, not moral (except perhaps for sexual psychopath laws), their use actually represents a decline in the moralistic conception of social problems. Discusion of psychiatric definitions is therefore delayed until examination of professional ideologies in Chapter 6. The expansion of psychiatric frames of reference is perhaps best conveyed in Peter Conrad and Joseph Schneider's, *Deviance and Medicalization: from Badness to Sickness*, St. Louis, Mo.: Mosby, 1980.
25. The same is true of movements like the Chartists of England and similar groups on the European Continent to extend the vote to the masses. See John

slavery movements of the nineteenth century had extremely close ties with organized religion—although there were religious advocates on both sides of the conflict. The nineteenth century socialist movements of Europe typically rejected conventional religion as hopelessly supportive of the economic status quo, and were likewise rejected by the established religions of the day.

In the twentieth century many churches developed (or possibly returned to) what has been called a *social gospel*.[26] As Allen put it,

> The social gospel rested on the premise that Christianity was a social religion, concerned ... with the quality of human relations on this earth. Put in more dramatic terms, it was a call for men to find the meaning of their lives in seeking ... the Kingdom of God in the very fabric of society.[27]

Many denominations of organized religion are today far more concerned with alleviating injustice and misery on earth than with saving souls from the torments of Hell. To be sure, both interests have always been visible, but the balance has shifted considerably in this century. From this shift comes the term, the social gospel.

The ambivalence of linkage between egalitarian movements and religious efforts continues. The recent civil rights movements for blacks in the United States was closely associated with the social gospel component of organized religion. The womens' liberation movement, on the other hand, has been completely separate, receiving more or less equal amounts of support and flak from religious sources. Because egalitarianism in its various manifestations has become a separate force in history (notwithstanding religious roots) and has in fact be-

Gwynne-Timothy, *Question for Democracy*, Vols. 1 and 2, Toronto: McClelland and Stewart, 1970.
26. C.H. Hopkins, *The Rise of the Social Gospel in American Protestantism, 1865-1915*, New Haven: Yale University Press, 1967.
27. A.R. Allen, *The Social Passion: Religion and Social Reform in Canada, 1914-1928*, Toronto: University of Toronto Press, 1971, p. 4.

come even stronger than organized religion in certain cases, it is best to treat it now in its own section.

EGALITARIAN ENTREPRENEURS

Sociologists have developed a tendency to speak of moral entrepreneurship with regard to activities they disapprove of, typically those motivated by business interests or fundamentalist Christianity. They reserve the labels "social reform" or "social movements" for legislative entrepreneurship they espouse, usually humanistic lawmaking. There is, certainly, a difference in the basis of the advocated changes—whether conservative or progressive—but not infrequently the activities of the advocates are highly similar. Sociologists themselves have been moral entrepreneurs with respect to advancing such notions as white-collar crime. In this chapter we consider both forms of moralistic legislation as cases of moral enterprising.

As seen in Chapter 2, a prominent feature of nineteenth and twentieth century thought has been the expansion of public consciousness and concern to include the suffering and inequities of ever-wider circles of society—circles for whom earlier generations considered suffering to be part of an escapable lot. The American and French Revolutions were, as many writers have observed, among the earliest indications of this expansion of compassion. But more to the point at hand are the numerous reform movements whose aims have been to expand suffrage and prohibit exploitation. The anti-slavery movements of Britain and the United States were undoubtedly among the greatest of such developments in the nineteenth century, alongside the emergence of the socialist movement in Europe. As the twentieth century began, the subordinate status of women became widely deplored; this was accompanied or followed by the rise of the trade union movement, government-backed security for the aged, the civil rights movement for blacks and Indians, independence for former colonies of Europe, and, most recently, anti-poverty campaigns and a rebirth of the women's rights movement. In each case, an inequitable condition formerly taken for granted as part of the natural and inescapable order of things suddenly assumed the status of a social problem. Again it is logical to ask who the definers have been with respect to these cultural transformations.

Typically, the active members of the afflicted group have served more as shock troops than as definers for society as a whole, even though dramatic actions have on occasion provided "propaganda of the deed" to help awaken a sleeping society. It is frequently the inarticulate, inchoate actions of desperate members of a disadvantaged group which first alert the more perceptive of the intellectuals to a sense of their plight.[28] But to see such actions as protest rather than as mindless deviance requires special interpreters: an intellectual vanguard. The first defining efforts have usually come from the unattached intellectual rather than from members of the downtrodden.[29] Of course the two categories are hardly mutually exclusive, and it is not surprising to find black intellectuals and academic women prominent in the movements of their respective groups and playing key roles in redefining familiar misery.[30] For blacks, Indians, women, and working-class sons to become members of the intelligentsia, however, there must first have been a break in the barriers within the educational system, allowing access to members of underprivileged segments of society.

28. Since the black ghetto riots of the 1960's there has been increased discussion of the latent functions of violence as a form of protest, of which the Luddites and Molly Maguires of the nineteenth century furnish some of the clearest examples. See, e.g., Ralph H. Turner, "The Public Perception of Protest," *American Sociological Review*, 34, 1969, pp. 815-831.

29. See Barry Krisberg, "The Sociological Imagination Revisited," *Canadian Journal of Criminology and Corrections*, 16, 1974, pp. 146-161. Eric Hoffer has envisaged social movements divided into stages, in the sense that the types of persons who excel in the first stage ("men of ideas") do not shine in later phases. Here, the "men of words" and then the "men of action" come into prominence. Rarely, says Hoffer, do we find these various roles filled by the same people. Eric Hoffer, *The True Believer: Thoughts on the Nature of Mass Movements*, New York: Harper & Row, 1951.

30. For such an example among Canadian Indians, we can refer to Harold Cardinal, author of *The Unjust Society: The Tragedy of Canada's Indians*, Edmonton: M.G. Hurtig, 1969.

OVERVIEW

The definitional aspect of the social problem label is seen most vividly with respect to crime, for crimes are those activities of social life which are most severely sanctioned, yet which some people wish to take part in. The legislators who make the criminal law must, therefore, decide which part of their constituencies they will listen to: the doers or the would-be preventers.

Several studies have investigated the active sponsorship of legislation and the personal backgrounds of the legislators. The equating of criminality with immorality by many persons does aid the moral entrepreneur when he or she succeeds in obtaining a new legal prohibition. In terms of enforceability, laws prohibiting victimless acts are the most vulnerable to abuse and corruption, and probably the most questionable aspects of the "law explosion." The study of moral entrepreneurship would be incomplete without a discussion of modern egalitarian social movements. There was not time here to examine in detail the origins or tactics of such groups, but the discussion served to secure their position as part of the definitional process.[31] Psychiatric conceptions as sources of social problem perspectives and definitions are examined Chapters 6 and 7.

---

31. Probably the best analysis of the origins and "natural histories" of social reform movements is contained in Armand L. Mauss, *Social Problems as Social Movements*, Philadelphia: Lippincott, 1975.

6 Defining Social Problems: The Intellectual and the Professional

> *It is strange that we have few men of genius on our faculties; we are always trying to get them. Of course they must have undergone the regular academic training (say ten years in graduate study and subordinate positions) and be gentlemanly, dependable, pleasant to live with, and not apt to make trouble by urging eccentric ideas.*
>
> —Charles Horton Cooley

It is not unusual in discussions of social problems to see moral entrepreneurs from the general population examined and subjected to a certain amount of ridicule. But these moral fundamentalists accomplish only a part of the definitional task respecting social problems; much of the remainder is performed by intellectuals—chiefly writers and academics—and by experts on social problems. And such special persons are not so commonly held up to criticism in terms of their definitional role.

In a dazzling reversal of fortune, intellectuals—for whom even the word "intellectual" itself formerly held negative connotations—are becoming people from whom solutions to social problems are expected. This provides them with considerable power to define where social problems lie. Only two decades ago the situation was quite different: intellectuals in North America led a strange life. On the one hand, as surveys showed, they were widely respected, and their social acceptability was among the highest of any occupational group.[1] Yet, in 1958, a widely cited study found among intellectuals a definite fear of displaying their own scholarly superiority. Not only in their public pronouncements but in anonymous surveys of their innermost feelings, minority-like responses were discovered which included acceptance of negative stereotypes of the intellectual (a remarkable level of "self-hate"), a marked concern over the deviant behaviour of a few intellectuals, and a suffocating approval of conforming behaviour.[2] Not only in these theoretical characteristics but even more in the concrete responses to specific questions did the intellectual of that time, shortly after the McCarthy era, sound strikingly different from the confident intellectual of today.

Today in some respects intellectuals have come to take the place which the clergy occupied in earlier centuries in the idolatry of the public. This is not to say that all quarters are pleased by this transformation, just as anti-clericalism existed in the days when the clergy was widely looked to for answers. And the public can readily believe that the intellectual makes mistakes, as anti-intellectuals delight in reminding us. But in spite of this, intellectual self-confidence has grown to the point that a new litany has emerged—startlingly new, yet already highly potent. It is a frankly elitist position, yet one espoused not only in some quarters of intellectualdom itself but also by admiring nonmembers, especially among the young of the early 1970's.

Turning to the position of the expert, the professional, there has been a growing acceptance by both the general public and by governmental authorities of the need for specialists in fields of social problems. There is increasing recognition of the presumed expertise of professionals and semi-professionals in several fields: criminologists, prison psychologists, social workers, sex therapists, marriage counsellors, psychiatrists, psychoanalysts, labour/management mediators, geriatric spe-

1. See Robert W. Hodge *et al.*, "Occupational Prestige in the United States: 1925-1963," in *Class, Status, and Power*, second edition, edited by Reinhard Bendix and Seymour M. Lipset, New York: Free Press, 1966.
2. Melvin Seeman, "The Intellectual and the Language of the Minorities," *American Journal of Sociology*, 64, 1958, pp. 25-35.

cialists, suicidologists—the list grows lengthy. In addition, one can detect increasing acceptance of training programmes; formal training for these areas grows in importance at the expense of skills learned on the job. In recent years there has been a burgeoning demand for college-level courses and programmes in skills relating to social problems. Although most of the specialities existed prior to their professionalization, newer fields are composed almost exclusively of professionals, in the traditional sense, including such emerging classifications as suicidology or conflict resolution.

THE CLAIMS OF THE INTELLECTUAL AND THE EXPERT

One aspect of the intellectuals' claim is anything but new; it follows the classical notion of "philosopher-king" first articulated over 2,000 years ago in Plato's *Republic*. In this perspective, intellectuals (Plato's "philosophers") are best suited to lead society because they know so much more than anyone else, not merely in factual matters but in terms of their sensing of underlying relationships, deep historical and international perspectives, and (perhaps) a wisdom that comes from a lifetime of reading and absorbing ideas. Associated with the recurring claim of the intellectual to unique qualifications for the role of philosopher-king is a newer claim, based on social science and allied disciplines, for what Lilienfeld has called the role of "scientist-king."[3] Some time ago one prominent sociologist depicted this latter claim as follows:

> *Modern social scientists . . . no longer believe that men can rid their minds of impediments to lucid thought: only scientists can. . . . They assert that there is only one escape from the consequences of irrationality: that is by the application of scientific method. And this method can be used effectively only by the expert few. . . . Instead of attempting to make*

3. Robert Lilienfeld, *The Rise of Systems Theory: An Ideological Perspective,* New York: Wiley, 1978, p. 3.

people more rational, contemporary social scientists often content themselves with asking of them that they place their trust in social science and accept its findings.[4]

The philosopher-king is a classical notion, and even his new cousin the scientist-king is by now a well established conceit. But now, in addition, comes a variation based upon an ongoing transformation of the modern world into what some have termed an "information society." In this new situation, upon which numerous observers have commented, the production and distribution of knowledge has been systematized and supported as never before; concurrently the *knowledge industry* assumes a centrality never before witnessed in history.

Whereas invention and discovery were formerly undertaken haphazardly, there has been, first, a gradual mating of science and technology and, more recently, the emergence of research and development as an industry in its own right. We are, as has been remarked, the first civilization to systematize the processes of innovation and discovery. (Alfred North Whitehead once noted that the greatest invention of the nineteenth century was the comprehension of the method of invention.) In North America research and development has become a multibillion dollar activity, with support coming not solely, or even primarily, from the university but also from government as well as business interests. After specific innovations appear, their rapid and smooth introduction into the mainstream of economic and social life has itself become an area with its own expertise. In addition to basic research and development, an enormous coterie of investigators keeps tabs on every facet of our ongoing economic condition, attitudes, and population characteristics. Throughout the Western world, then, this knowledge industry is today one of the largest economic units, and growing even larger.[5]

4. Reinhard Bendix, "The Image of Man in the Social Sciences: The Basic Assumptions of Present-Day Research," *Commentary*, 11, 1951, pp. 187-192. Quoted is page 190.
5. For an excellent overview of the production, organization, distribution, application, and utilization of technical knowledge in the modern world, see Burkart Holzner and John A. Marx, *Knowledge Application: The Knowledge System in Society*, Boston: Allyn and Bacon, 1979.

Numerous scholars have forecast that the production of knowledge will be the most important institution in the emerging "post-industrial," "post-modern," "technocratic" society. According to Daniel Bell, the creation and utilization of theoretical knowledge will become the central, axial principle of society, with decision-making itself the subject of an intellectual technology run by technocrats.[6] As a result of these trends, and the concomitant occupational shifts, some have seen the professional and technical class emerging as the dominant occupational group in the post-industrial society, with a commanding role to be played by scientists, professionals, and technocrats.

Let us review momentarily what John Kenneth Galbraith told us in 1967 about the rise of a new estate and what should be done with the power it grants. The elitist connotations are difficult to ignore: the academicians know best, and they now possess power:

> *The requirements of technology and planning have greatly increased the need of the industrial enterprise for specialized talent and for its organization. The industrial system must rely, in the main, on external sources for this talent. Unlike capital it is not something that the firm can supply to itself.... The mere possession of capital is now no guarantee that the requisite talent can be obtained and organized. One should expect, from past experience, to find a new shift of power in the industrial enterprise, this one from capital to organized intelligence. And one would expect that this shift would be reflected in the deployment of power in the society at large ... it has been disguised because power has not gone to another of the established factors as they are celebrated in conventional economic pedagogy. It has not passed to labor. ... Power has, in fact, passed to what anyone in search of novelty might be justified in calling a new factor of production ... Most directly nurtured by the industrial system are the*

6. Daniel Bell, *The Coming of Post-Industrial Society*, New York: Basic Books, 1973. This theme—that knowledge production will be the major trait of our future society—has also been well developed by Peter F. Drucker in *The Age of Discontinuity*, New York: Harper and Row, 1969.

educators and scientists in the schools, colleges, universities and research institutions. They stand in relation to the industrial systems much as did the banking and financial community to the earlier stages of industrial development.... And the values and attitudes of the society have been appropriately altered to reinforce the change.[7]

Galbraith is describing a situation that has also interested other writers. Lipset points out that

Modern societies—both Communist and non-Communist—face a growing dilemma posed by the fact that key institutions and their elites are increasingly dependent upon intellectuals. ... Yet, the leaders in these [intellectual groupings] are among the major critics of the way in which the society operates, sometimes calling into question the legitimacy of the social order.... A ruling elite, even one that is conservative and anti-intellectual, cannot respond to such challenges by crushing the intellectuals, unless it is willing to incur the punitive costs which such repression entails.[8]

As David Bazelon puts it, "The intellectuals are coming on. They are increasingly strong, confident, and assertive. They know they are needed—and they are in fact needed more and more every day."[9] What does Galbraith make of this phenomenon?

Education ... has now the greatest solemnity of social purpose. ... With the rise of the technostructure, relations between those associated with economic enterprise and the educational and scientific estate undergo a radical transformation. ... At this stage, the educational and scientific estate is no longer small; on the contrary, it is very large. It is no longer dependent on private income and wealth for its

7. John Kenneth Galbraith, The New Industrial State, Boston: Houghton Mifflin, 1967, pp. 57-58. For a similar argument see Drucker, ibid.
8. Seymour Martin Lipset and Richard B. Dobson, "The Intellectual as Critic and Rebel: With Special Reference to the United States and the Soviet Union," Daedalus, 101, 1972, pp. 137-198. Quote is from p. 137.
9. David T. Bazelon, The Paper Economy, New York: Vintage Books, 1965, p. 319.

support; most of its sustenance is provided by the state. ...
Meanwhile the technostructure has become deeply dependent on the educational and scientific estate for its supply of
trained manpower.... The educational and scientific estate is
... growing rapidly in numbers. It still lacks a sense of its own
identity. It has also sat for many years under the shadow of
entrepreneurial power. ... Yet it is possible that the educational and scientific estate requires only a strongly creative
political hand to become a decisive instrument of political
power.[10]

Finally the message is clear: the university is relatively invulnerable. What does this mean to Galbraith?

The proper course of action is clear. The college and university community must retain paramount authority for the
education it provides and for the research it undertakes. The
needs of the industrial system must always be secondary to
the cultivation of general understanding and perception. ...
The educational and scientific estate has the power to
exercise its option. It holds the critical cards. For in committing itself to technology, planning and organization, the
industrial system has made itself deeply dependent on the
manpower which these require. The banker, in the days when
capital was decisive, was not unaware of his bargaining
power. The educator should not be more innocent today.[11]

The words are beguiling, and who could argue in the abstract
with what he wishes for the university?[12] Yet the Galbraith
proposal must be regarded in many respects as a manifesto.
Indeed one journal, in reprinting certain sections, used the
subtitle: "Educators of the World Unite!"[13]

10. Galbraith, *op. cit.*, pp. 288-9; 294-5.
11. *Ibid.*, pp. 372; 376.
12. Also, many of the deeds Galbraith has claimed academicians have already
achieved with their new power seem very worth doing. See his "An Adult's
Guide to New York, Washington and Other Exotic Places," *New York*,
November 15, 1971, p. 52.
13. *Current*, October, 1969, p. 19. For an equally beguiling view of the
responsibilities—and the capacities—of academic man, see Walter Lippmann,
"The University," *The New Republic*, May 28, 1966, pp. 17-20.

The various claims of special enlightenment advanced on behalf of intellectuals and professionals raise a number of issues. First, the analyses of Galbraith and others seem to say that increased power for the knowledge industry is virtually inevitable—that, in fact, the industry will unavoidably become the single most powerful sector through some sort of structural necessity. But Anthony Giddens points out that this confuses indispensability and power: "if being indispensable necessarily confers power, then in a slave economy the slaves would be dominant."[14] A second issue is whether, empirically, increased power is indeed presently flowing to the knowledge sector. To examine this issue in depth here would take us too far off our course, but interested readers can look at the affirmative answers provided by Kleinberg, Lowi, and others.[15] The third issue takes us out of the realm of fact (or theory) in order to examine a normative issue: *should* the knowledge sector be accorded a special status in view of its claims? The remainder of this chapter will look critically at this question in terms of one major aspect: the influences and pressures that create distortion in perspectives on social problems arising from intellectuals and professionals. We will examine, consecutively, the effects of common origins and experiences, ambitions and peer pressures, institutional pressures, and professional ideologies, in the shaping of intellectual and expert viewpoints. One form of expert opinion on social problems, that of the psychiatric community, is sufficiently important that it will receive special attention in a final separate section.

COMMON EXPERIENCES AND ORIGINS OF INTELLECTUALS

In contrast to the above endorsements of academia's power role, Eric Hoffer, the longshoreman-philosopher, has castigated intellectuals for being out of touch with the people. Indeed there

14. Anthony Giddens, *The Class Structure of the Advanced Societies*, London: Hutchinson, 1973, p. 173. See also his comments on pp. 195-6, 256-7, and 262-3.
15. Benjamin Kleinberg, *American Society in the Postindustrial Age*, Columbus, Ohio: Merrill, 1973; Theodore J. Lowi, *The End of Liberalism—Ideology, Policy, and the Crisis of Public Authority*, New York: Norton, 1969.

seems to be an unavoidable dilemma here: if we adopt the sociology of knowledge perspective, the views people hold are derived not only from a logical analysis of facts but from their own life experiences. If intellectuals are persons who make their way exchanging ideas, then their life experiences will be circumscribed by the world of literature, criticism, and scholarship. As Anderson and Murray put it, "Academics work with ideas, concepts, abstract relationships, and theories about people and things, more than they do with people and things."[16] Some academics have spent their entire adult lives in the university. In short, their expertise and proficiency with ideas will be great but their common experiences will tend to provoke a common world view, which may or may not be in the best interest of the rest of society.

Correspondence of background can apply not only to the professional lives and shared experiences of intellectuals but also to their social origins. There is a self-selection process at work in recruiting for most occupations, and intellectualdom is no exception to such occupational selection. Persons with certain personalities or values are attracted to such a life; others are repelled by it. As one striking example of this, over half of the early American sociologists had a ministerial background, and even today an unusually high percentage once considered entering the clergy.[17] (We sometimes seem to concentrate on sociologists, but only because more is known about them than about other academicians.)[18] Bell and Mau suggest that social scientists usually come from similar backgrounds, and thus share similar biases.[19] These similar experiences in both pro-

16. Charles H. Anderson and John D. Murray, eds., *The Professors*, Cambridge: Schenkman, 1971, p. 185. See also Paul F. Lazarsfeld and W. Thielens, Jr., *The Academic Mind*, Glencoe, Ill.: Free Press, 1958.

17. Roscoe C. Hinkle and Gisela J. Hinkle, *The Development of Modern Sociology*, New York: Random House, 1962; Alvin W. Gouldner, *The Coming Crisis of Western Sociology*, New York: Basic Books, 1970, p. 24.

18. For several articles on the conscious and unconscious value premises affecting the findings of sociologists, see the last section of *The Sociology of Sociology*, edited by Larry T. Reynolds and Janice M. Reynolds, New York: McKay, 1970.

19. Wendell Bell and James A. Mau, "Images of the Future: Theory and Research Strategies," in *The Sociology of the Future*, edited by W. Bell and J.A. Mau, New York: Russell Sage, 1971.

fessional and earlier life can scarcely avoid producing certain tendencies in thinking—in particular, we suspect, in thinking about social problems. It has often been suggested that academia attracts young persons with liberal-left views because the vast majority of academics hold such views, while equally intelligent young persons with other beliefs move into different occupations.

There is another aspect to occupational selection that operates here: selection into intellectualdom is based in large part on formal education attainments, a fact which further narrows the possible base of recruitment. Then too, of course, the education that is a requisite for the intellectual life constitutes by itself yet another variety of shared experience which all members have in common, thus shaping a more uniform world view.

Anderson conducted a study of the friendship patterns of academic intellectuals, with striking results. He found that most academics virtually restricted their friends to other professors.[20] The number of non-academic friends was small not only in an absolute sense but also in comparison to the number of friends outside the in-group found among members of other professions (e.g., lawyers and engineers). With the further revelation that academics maintain very few ties with their kin and—except for other professors—very few neighbourhood ties, the *isolation* of academicians in terms of interpersonal experiences is evident. In Anderson's words, "Neither clique, kin, neighborhood, nor club acted as a social bridge to surrounding society."[21]

Such self-imposed isolation is not without its benefits in certain cases, but in terms of understanding and empathizing with everyday citizens, and of reordering society for their benefit, the disadvantages are painfully clear. Perhaps relatedly, research on empathy—although of somewhat limited scope—seems to show consistently that social scientists are somewhat *less* competent in judging persons than lay individ-

20. Charles H. Anderson, "Marginality and the Academic," in *The Professors, op. cit.*, p. 210.
21. *Ibid.* The physical isolation of university towns and the concentration of scholars in cosmopolitan cities may also facilitate a breakdown of contact. See Lipset and Dobson, *op. cit.*, pp. 161-2 and 192.

uals without professional training.[22] After an exhaustive review of such studies, one researcher concluded that "It is astounding that judges and correctional officials continue to view psychiatrists as experts on human behavior when there is considerable experimental evidence and other research which shows laymen superior to psychiatrists ... in the judgment of people's motives, abilities, personality traits, and action tendencies."[23]

Clearly, values and general orientations influence researchers' choice of specialization, and also their choice of specific research topics.

C. Wright Mills long ago uncovered one unconscious tendency of American sociology.[24] Pointing out the predominantly rural backgrounds of most sociologists of the day, he also saw certain rural values being interjected into their professional writings. Prominent among these was a distrust of the characteristics of modern urban society and a longing for the return of the values of the small community. This nostalgia for a "return to community" was understandable in terms of the backgrounds of the writers, but it apparently led to a position in which the cultural patterns of the metropolis were seen as inherently pathological.[25] The gross over-extension of the idea of "social disorganization" to all slum areas by early sociological observers was one consequence of this orientation, although it was based on other misconceptions as well.[26]

22. See, e.g., R. Taft, "The Ability to Judge People," *Psychological Bulletin*, 52, 1955, pp. 1-23; M. Hakeem, "A Critique of the Psychiatric Approach to Crime and Corrections," *Law and Contemporary Problems*, 23, 1958, p. 650-682.

23. Hakeem, *ibid.*, p. 682. Taft surveyed some 81 studies in coming to his conclusion. His analysis has been updated by Theodore Sarbin, R. Taft, and D.E. Bailey, *Clinical Inference and Cognitive Theory*, New York: Holt, 1960, with little if any change in the conclusions.

24. C. Wright Mills, "The Professional Ideology of Social Pathologists," in *Power, Politics and People*, by C. Wright Mills, edited by Irving L. Horowitz, New York: Ballantine Books, 1963 (original: 1943), pp. 525-552.

25. Of course, there may be some truth to this assumption, as the Midtown Manhattan Study would appear to indicate. (Leo Srole *et al.*, *Mental Health in the Metropolis*, New York: McGraw Hill, 1962). But no such clear-cut basis was at the heart of the writings Mills examined.

26. For discussion of the concept of social disorganization in this regard, see Chapter 3, and Richard A. Coward and Lloyd E. Ohlin, *Delinquency and Opportunity*, New York: Free Press, 1966, pp. 154-159.

The background and self-imposed social isolation of intellectuals impacts on their values, and sometimes the values of researchers impact on their conclusions in very direct ways. At various times academic sociologists have tended to view some social problems in a favourable light, or at least with benign complacency. Currently, for example, divorce is one such problem with relatively favoured status.[27] In her review of the literature on the effect of divorce on children, Ambert found an exaggerated optimism on the part of sociologists—an optimism not shared by clinicians, psychologically oriented researchers or her own data.[28] In general such tendencies derive not from distortion of research findings (such would violate norms of objectivity) but from decisions to investigate thoroughly certain aspects of a problem to the detriment of others. Liberals, for example, can focus on the indignities suffered by welfare recipients; conservatives can focus on welfare cheating.

MOTIVATIONS AND AMBITIONS OF INTELLECTUALS

The ministerial underpinnings of modern sociologists should prepare us for what some observers have seen as a need of the intellectual for service to humanity.[29] Hoffer, for instance, has maintained that a true utopia would be the worst possible place for intellectuals—in the perfect society they would have nothing to do. For Hoffer, the greatest need of the intellectual is to feel needed—disliked, perhaps, but essential. This theme is echoed in the first part of Milosz's *The Captive Mind*, in which

27. Bohannan refers to Tumin's analysis in his Introduction to *Divorce and After*, edited by P. Bohannan, New York: Doubleday, 1970, pp. 9-10.
28. Anne-Marie Ambert, *Divorce in Canada*, Toronto: Academic Press Canada, 1980, p. 166, and "Differences in Children's Behavior Toward Custodial Mothers and Custodial Fathers," *Journal of Marriage and the Family*, 44, 1982, pp. 73-86. See also J.S. Wallerstein and J.B. Kelly, *Surviving the Breakup*, New York: Basic Books, 1980; C. Longfellow, "Divorce in Context: Its Impact on Children," in *Divorce and Separation*, edited by G. Levinger and O.C. Moles, New York: Basic Books, 1979.
29. For a synopsis of the reformist character of early American sociology, see Lewis A. Coser, *The Functions of Social Conflict*, New York: Free Press, 1966, pp. 16-18.

he maintained that the need to feel needed has been the driving force behind the attraction of intellectuals to otherwise distasteful doctrines.[30] Killian detects an unrecognized streak of "optimism" in both liberal and radical sociological writings: a belief that all social problems are inherently solvable. Radical and liberal sociologists disagree on methods of resolution, but both seem to believe that all social problems *can* be solved.[31] Yet, outside of sociological literature (which Killian sees as old-fashioned in this sense), there is an increasing pessimism about society's ability to solve the problems that confront it.

It may be objected that we are castigating the intelligentsia for what are really laudable habits, but such is not the intention. Intellectuals are a potent force in the definitional process today, perhaps *the* important force, and an examination of even their commendable motivations is therefore obligatory. In addition, there are unfortunately other forces at work which can under no interpretation be considered desirable.

Despite traditional values which decry self-serving motivations, intellectuals are frequently seized by ambition, perhaps as frequently as anyone else in their competitive society. The desire of intellectuals for good works notwithstanding, it is perhaps the degree to which they must guard against an open admission of their thirst for fame, power, and wealth which most clearly differentiates them from other professions.[32] It is true that wealth is rarely obtainable, even though intellectuals have long outgrown the cloak of poverty they once suffered under and protected themselves with.[33] But the search for the remaining objectives, fame and power, is quite sufficient to channel writers' expressions, and perhaps their thought, into lines acceptable to the others whom they must impress.

---

30. Eric Hoffer, *The True Believer: Thoughts on the Nature of Mass Movements*, New York: Mentor, 1951; Czeslaw Milosz, *The Captive Mind*, translated by Jane Zielonko, New York: Vintage Books, 1957.
31. Lewis M. Killian, "Optimism and Pessimism in Sociological Analysis," *American Sociologist*, 6, 1971, pp. 281-286.
32. Podhoretz speaks at length on this norm of concealment, and how it continues to operate long after the virtues it is supposed to protect have vanished. Norman Podhoretz, *Making It*, New York: Random House, 1967.
33. Anderson and Murray, *op. cit.*, pp. 7-8.

How can pervasive ambition be demonstrated when the norms so strongly militate against its outward manifestation? One way is through indirect evidence. Merton, for example, has studied the ways in which scientists have guarded their intellectual property against "theft" by other scientists.[34] The lengths and measures which he catalogs are extraordinarily clear indicators of the workings of personal ambition, as are the cries of anguish and outrage when an idea is stolen in spite of precautions.[35] We can also open a window on ambition through the pressure-free writings of persons who have already made it, and feel an urge to describe their part of the intellectual world as it really appears to them. Thus Podhoretz, in his book appropriately titled *Making It*, describes his early ambivalence toward power and his clear desire for fame, which led him into certain ventures for purely careerist reasons.[36] And in place of the public affectation of surprise and delight when one receives the Nobel Prize, Watson tells honestly of deliberately setting the Prize as his goal, and of engaging in an open race to uncover the structure of DNA to obtain it. A similarly revealing account is provided by Johanson and Edey of the personal rivalries, ambitions, and devious calculations in the outwardly stiff scientific race presently underway by paleoanthropologists to discover the *earliest* of early man in the valleys of East Africa.[37]

Insofar as ambition and enlightenment are in harmony there is no need for criticism; the negative side of ambition appears whenever assuming a certain position in one's work will damage one's career chances. Here workers in the humanities and social sciences are far more vulnerable than physical scientists and mathematicians, both because modern society tends to divorce physical laws from ideology,[38] and because the

---

34. Robert K. Merton, "Priorities in Scientific Discovery: A Chapter in the Sociology of Science," *American Sociological Review*, 22, 1959, pp. 635-659.
35. To be sure, our concentration on negative features displays only part of the total picture, for personal ambition often works to the benefit of science.
36. Podhoretz, *op. cit.*
37. James D. Watson, *The Double Helix*, New York: New American Library, 1969; Donald Johanson and Maitland Edey, *Lucy: The Beginnings of Humankind*, New York: Simon and Schuster, 1981.
38. It was not always thus. Even today the separation is incomplete, as an investigation of the affairs of Lysenko and Velikovsky will confirm. See D. Joravsky, "Lysenkoism," *Scientific American*, 207, November, 1962, pp. 41-49;

worth of a contribution is more readily ascertainable in the physical and formal sciences.[39]

The traditional way to view the vulnerability of intellectuals has been in terms of pressures from the larger society, e.g., the witch hunts of a Senator McCarthy. However, in terms of career progress, the opinion of one's peers has infinitely more control over one's destiny than the opinion of the non-intellectual world—and rightly so. Moral cowardice among intellectuals can thus occur not only in a reluctance to attack, expose, or condemn the larger society. These actions may be done as a matter of routine—even a mandatory routine—in some circles. Lionel Trilling has coined the term "adversary culture" to speak of the feeling of obligation in some intellectual circles to be critical of society.[40] Cowardice lies also in a well-grounded fear that attacking beliefs cherished by one's colleagues spells defeat for all ordinary ambitions. Thus intellectuals commend each other for their bravery in attacking the society at large, when in point of fact it would in many quarters require greater courage not to do so.[41] Equally great respect must be accorded to those intellectuals who have dared, on matters of great importance, to fight their peers even at the risk of ostracism. No political persuasion apparently monopolizes this rare phenomenon—C. Wright Mills was further to the political left than his colleagues; Thomas Szasz, the disturber of psychiatry, is

---

Eric Larrabee, "Scientists in Collision: Was Velikovsky Right?" *Harper's*, 227, August, 1963, pp. 48-55. See also Marian Blissett, *Politics in Science*, Boston: Little, Brown, 1972.

39. To demonstrate this, we might consider a situation in which the Nobel Prize was extended to sociology. It seems safe to say that a twenty-four-year-old sociologist with no prior publications simply could not obtain it, but Watson received it in the field of biology for his decoding of the DNA molecule while at that age and condition. The youngest laureate in the sciences received his prize at the age of 25; the youngest laureate in the humanities was 41.

40. See his *Beyond Culture*, New York: Viking Press, 1965, pp. xii-xiii.

41. The term "new class" was invented in the early 1970's to refer to those who made it an obligation, a mandatory routine, to condemn the contemporary social order. The "paradox" that interested researchers was that such groups and individuals, supporting radical change, were invariably well-off, even privileged, while those who defended the status quo were typically poor, even downtrodden. See *The New Class?*, edited by B. Bruce-Briggs, New Brunswick, N.J.: Transaction Books, 1979.

apparently to the right of this. The weight of the system militates heavily against this type of independent "counterformity."[42]

Intellectuals succeed in publishing if they meet the overt criteria of quality and stay within covert boundaries of ideology set by their colleagues.[43] Already therefore, there is a requisite degree of conformity to the norms of the profession.[44] Then, after publishing, in order to advance professionally (hirings, chairmanships, editorial roles), and even to be accepted in the professional hierarchy, they have again to submit repeatedly to the judgment of their peers. The occupational viewpoints that emerge can therefore be stabilized by group censure for participation in disapproved experiences (the military, for example) or in writing disapproved literature, and further stabilized by psychological mechanisms: selective exposure to new ideas, selective perception, and selective retention.[45] Long ago, Charles Horton Cooley summarized the situation with an aphorism that might have been written yesterday. Taken from his *Life and the Student*, it is the epigraph at the beginning of the chapter. Cooley first deplores the scarcity of genius in the university and then, as if by accident, he juxtaposes the real-world requirements for acceptance and acceptability. The

42. What we are referring to must be distinguished from other forms of "acceptable" criticism of colleagues. There seem to be safe and unsafe areas of criticism, and, if we may draw from Reisman's old Lonely Crowd imagery, the intellectual seems to possess a delicate radar for detecting the forbidden areas, those beyond the pale. See in this regard, with respect to the Nobel Prize in science, William K. Stuckey, "The Prize," *Saturday Review*, September 2, 1972, pp. 33-39. In safe areas, on the other hand, there is actually a premium on original criticism.

43. See Nan Lin, "Stratification of the Formal Communication System in Science," paper presented at the annual meeting of the American Sociological Association, Denver, Colorado, August, 1971; Diana Crane, "Scientists at Major and Minor Universities: A Study of Productivity and Recognition," *American Sociological Review*, 32, 1965, pp. 377-390; and her "The Gate-keepers of Science: Some Factors Affecting the Selection of Articles for Scientific Journals," *American Sociologist*, 2, 1967, pp. 195-201.

44. See James B. McKee, "Some Observations on the Self Consciousness of Sociologists," in *The Sociology of Sociology, op. cit.*

45. See the literature on these strong tendencies reviewed in Joseph T. Klapper, *The Effects of Mass Communication*, New York: Free Press, 1960, pp. 19-25 and 64-65; Bernard Berelson and Gary F. Steiner, *Human Behavior: An Inventory of Scientific Findings*, New York: Harcourt, 1964, pp. 529-533.

tension is real: faculties do try to get creative individuals; they simultaneously discourage wave-makers.

The strains of ambition lead also to other negative consequences for the intellectually honest study of social problems. They lead, for instance, to what some have called empire building: the erection of a research empire as a basis for personal power. To a considerable extent social research is dependent on foundation and governmental grant support.[46] Grants for research, especially large awards, are matters of prestige and power, eagerly sought. Because of this the conclusions reached in a sponsored study can at times be predicted with ease: to better secure the next grant, in the delicate nuances of grantsmanship, results will be pleasing to the granting agency, in line with the expectations and values of its directors. Simon concludes, for instance, that there is an incentive for scholars and institutions to produce bad news about overpopulation, resources, and environment, and to downplay good news, in terms of getting continued funding of their work.[47] Both private and public funding sources tend to avoid topics in which conclusions could inspire public controversy or subject the agency to criticism. Topics that remain permanently unfunded tend to be under-studied. This is understandable but regrettable; research efforts typically focus on less controversial subjects, irrespective of their theoretical or humane importance.[48]

> On occasion the research bureau's members are painfully surprised at the unanticipated reception of their endeavors. However, from such experience they learn much—what is absolutely safe, what is questionable, what is risky, what is dangerous, what is fatal. . . . The selection of additional or replacement personnel comes to be predicated not solely on

46. In this connection Gouldner maintains that, historically, the avoidance of radical schemes for social reconstruction was the admission price early sociologists paid for academic respectability. Alvin W. Gouldner, *op. cit.*, pp. 135-137.

47. Julian J. Simon, "Resources, Population, Environment: An Oversupply of False Bad News," *Science*, 208, June 27, 1980, pp. 1431-1437.

48. Of course what is controversial for educated persons in one era is no longer so in another, and research on hitherto forbidden topics therefore does occur.

*talent or demonstrated skill, but on the individual's capacity
to subordinate scientific concerns to institutional needs. . . .
Only those outsiders willing to take the vows of conformity,
or whose regularity is so transparent as to require no proof,
are admitted to the order. The "enthusiast" . . . is subordinated
to the bureaucrat.*[49]

Then too, these topics for which funding is provided *do* get
investigated. Monies earmarked for research on particular
subjects hardly ever go begging, irrespective of the relative
merit of funded and non-funded projects. Raymond Mack has
called this the "inverse Midas effect" for sociologists—"all that
turns to gold, they touch."[50] One important instance of this in the
social sciences was Project Camelot, a development of the
1960's in which the U.S. Army made a concerted effort through
a research institute (or "Office") to harness international social
science expertise to solve a social problem as the U.S. Army saw
it: the outbreak of hostile leftist regimes in Latin America.[51] The
fact that social scientists flocked in great numbers to this
project before it was cancelled illustrates Mack's point. The
detrimental consequences for a clear picture of the state of
social problems posed by lucrative financing imbalances
should be obvious.

In addition to a reluctance to displease granting agencies,
there is as well a decline in integrity stemming from the
necessity for the researcher to maintain good relations with the
individuals or groups being studied, especially if these groups
have a high degree of solidarity. Contacts highly desirable for
future investigations, such as those requiring participant observation, might be curtailed or jeopardized by hostile reactions to forthright, objective reporting. Similarly, ongoing
research might be prematurely terminated. One arena in which

49. Wilson Record, "Some Reflections on Bureaucratic Trends in Sociological
Research," *American Sociological Review*, 25, 1960, pp. 411-414. Quoted is
page 413.
50. Raymond W. Mack, "Theoretical and Substantive Biases in Sociological
Research," in *Interdisciplinary Relationships in the Social Sciences*, edited by
M. and C. Sherif, Chicago: Aldine, 1969.
51. Although the project was well advanced before discovery, the resultant
uproar crushed the project decisively.

this is highly relevant to social problems is observation of police forces. Police have an extraordinarily high degree of internal solidarity (vis-a-vis outsiders), and numerous reports have surfaced detailing the difficulties of doing objective reporting of police (including malpractices) while yet maintaining ties for future research.[52] In fact, overcoming this problem while observing any part of the criminal justice system, such as jury deliberations or plea bargaining, has proven extremely difficult.[53]

INSTITUTIONAL PRESSURES

The effects of ambition associated with empire building and grantsmanship shade gradually and imperceptibly into institutional pressures that affect all but the most independent self-employed. In addition to the effects of background and ambition, intellectual perspectives are also influenced by pressures from institutions with which most writers and scholars affiliate. Practically speaking this means primarily universities and research institutes.

From its position as a presumed bastion of intellectual integrity, the university has come under increasingly close scrutiny. In earlier decades, the university resolutely defended academic freedom against direct threats of encroachment which threatened to stifle the free expression of ideas. Even today there is no comparable sector of society so tolerant of strange or dissenting views, and this condition is jealously guarded by the academy. But present-day incursions are more insidious in nature, less a head-on clash with explicit insistence on intellectual conformity than a "flanking attack" posed by subtle changes in institutional structure. In one examination of this trend, Ralph Miliband listed four growing threats or constraints to the university's capacity for independent thinking. First, corporations are increasingly using the universities as

52. See R.J. Lundman and J.C. Fox, "Maintaining Research Access in Police Organizations," *Criminology*, 16, 1978, pp. 87-97, and the several sources cited.
53. See George J. McCall, *Observing the Law: Field Methods in the Study of Crime and the Criminal Justice System*, New York: Collier Macmillan, 1978.

consultants, encouraging, for payment, a reasonable view toward and understanding of business problems. Second, the university is directly supported to a substantial degree by corporations and wealthy individuals. This discourages views that would upset financial promotion and fund raising. Third, the controllers of the university (variously known as governors, regents, trustees) are drawn from persons of upper-class origin or the business elite. The fourth factor is that the business world is increasingly using the university as a training ground for future employees and administrators, including the by now well established phenomenon of whole faculties of business administration.[54] None of these intrusions is overwhelming, but subtle pressures are increasingly apparent.

Outside the university, the audience for social or economic research often provides more than grants or consultantships; frequently it acts as an outright employer as well. Many observers have commented that systems of patronage of science—including both governmental and corporate sponsorship—have steadily expanded in the twentieth century, accompanied by a commensurate decline in academic control.[55] Whereas in earlier periods sociology and psychology were almost wholly academic disciplines, the last few decades have witnessed the rise of applied psychology and sociology, with a small but growing number of professionals directly employed by governmental or institutional sponsors.[56] These traditionally academic disciplines are thus no longer quite so remote from the condition of economics, in which large numbers of graduates fill both academic and business or government positions.

To some extent the implications of this situation for perspectives on social problems parallels those found with the supporting grant, mentioned earlier, with the same general difficulties. But in addition those applied workers in the setting of the

54. Ralph Miliband, The State in Capitalist Society, New York: Quartet Books, 1975, especially pp. 224-226.
55. See, e.g., the discussion in Ron Johnston and Dave Robbins, "The Development of Specialties in Industrialized Science," The Sociological Review, 25, (New Series), 1977.
56. As one indicator of this trend, there is now a Section on Sociological Practice in the American Sociological Association.

research institute or think tank have to a great extent lost the freedom to choose their own topics of research, substituting the needs of their clients for what might have interested them on theoretical grounds. The sociologist or psychologist who affiliates with public or private bureaucracies will be expected to deal with problems as the decision-maker/employer sees them. And these are likely to concern the preservation or expansion of existing institutional arrangements.

The point is not to much that a number of individual researchers are diverted from their favourite topics but that distortions (via over- and under-emphases) develop in the knowledge of an entire field via the industrialization and politicization of its work. Blissett has charged that this type of scientific technostructure leads to a form of science "not committed to discovery or service to society, but rather to projects or programming aimed at accumulating and developing institutional resources."[57] Similarily, Johnston and Robbins have maintained that major "patrons" not only engender loyalty from their professional personnel but can also in the long run actually *create new specialties* in a discipline to satisfy their presumed needs as they alone define them.[58]

PROFESSIONAL IDEOLOGIES

If the temptations noted above apply for scholars not directly associated with a particular school of thought for the solution of a social problem, how much greater is the difficulty in avoiding bias for those professionals with an established interest in a particular problem. Here the aforementioned ambition is aligned with a feeling of team solidarity; what is good for individual career advancement is also good for a group in whose efforts one believes. Professionalism is not without numerous virtues, but it has often been noted that professions develop vested interests in the maintenance of a status quo. This does not mean that they do not attack problems, but that they perpetuate existing definitions of problematic areas as well as

---

57. Marian Blissett, *Politics in Science, op. cit.,* p. 195.
58. Johnston and Robbins, *op. cit.,* p. 90.

traditional perspectives and methods of dealing with them. Ultimately they may develop what Veblen called a trained incapacity to observe or deal with a situation in non-traditional ways. The helping professions thus at times present a paradoxical picture of institutions with liberal intentions which, through resistance to innovation, perpetuate the very problems they are involved in removing.[59] Put differently, professionals can be genuinely interested in helping but are over-committed to an established approach to social problems. The usual claim—that the present approach would succeed if only there were more professionals or more funds available—may indeed be true. Just where such beliefs fade into cynicism and empire-building for its own sake is sometimes difficult to discern.[60]

There is no space to evaluate all the claims and counter-claims about professional ideologies. At one time or another the specializations of industrial sociology, personality measurement, and motivational psychology have been singled out as the "servants of power".[61] These same fields have at times employed a "problem" framework which amply demonstrates the flexibility of this concept. Thus the Mayo School of industrial sociology felt that the principal source of labour difficulties involved a specific problem: breakdown of communication. The proposed means of resolution involved more adequate training of management in human relations approaches to its employees. The possibility of an inherent conflict of interest between labour and management, which clearer communication would only intensify, was scarcely considered as an alternative.[62]

59. With respect to labeling, the paradox may be even greater. See Thomas Scheff, *Being Mentally Ill*, Chicago: Aldine, 1966. For a general consideration of the role of the expert in social problem resolution see Chapter 5 of Richard L. Henshel, *Reacting to Social Problems*, Toronto: Academic Press Canada, 1976.
60. Herbert Gans points out that one of the functions of a social problem is to provide employment for persons who are supposed to solve it. Insofar as they are successful they literally work their way out of a job. See Herbert Gans, "The Positive Functions of Poverty," *American Journal of Sociology*, 78, 1972, pp. 275-289.
61. See especially Martin L. Gross, *The Brain Watchers*, New York: Random House, 1962, and Loren Baritz, *The Servants of Power*, New York: Wiley, 1965. At one time or another all academic disciplines have been accused of complicity with the "establishment." The fields mentioned in the text are especially vulnerable to this change.
62. For the other side, see Ralf Dahrendorf, *Class and Class Conflict in*

In the same manner, the use of personality testing and personnel classification in industry has been rationalized as helping to overcome the problem of unhappiness which results from improper job assignment. Yet the techniques of personality testing, at least as they have been applied in corporate settings, have been of highly dubious worth and validity, to say the least. In addition they seem to create new problems by discriminating inadvertently against minority applicants.[63] As for the use of motivational psychology in advertising, even its staunchest apologists have been hard-pressed in recent years to describe its work as beneficial to society, although such was not the case in earlier years with a different list of "problems."[64]

Other professional groups less subject to contemporary political criticism have displayed a similar tenacity in maintaining traditional views of what constitute social problems. Marriage counsellors have been castigated for their strict adherence to old norms respecting family patterns and sex roles.[65] Psychiatrists have seemingly learned little from the definitional critiques of Szasz and the labeling school, and psychoanalysts still less from numerous criticisms of their methods and perspectives.

PSYCHIATRIC DEFINITIONS

Contemporary psychiatry constitutes one of the strongest and most rapidly expanding bases for defining social problems. Here again it is instructive to examine the personal backgrounds and ideological leanings of the definers, with the important addition that the very basis for the authority of these key individuals is under attack from within.[66]

Industrial Society, Stanford: Stanford University Press, 1959 (Part 2).

63. Gross, *op. cit.*, examines the misuse of personality tests in great detail. A host of further debunking references are listed in Baritz, *op. cit.*, pp. 243-244.

64. Gross, *ibid.*

65. Paul Halmos, *The Faith of the Counsellors*, Don Mills, Ontario: Longman, 1965.

66. See Edwin M. Schur, "Psychiatrists Under Attack, The Rebellious Dr. Szasz," *The Atlantic*, June, 1966, pp. 72-76. Szasz stood virtually alone at first,

It is an old realization that psychiatry needs patients, not only for purposes of employment but in order to socially validate its role. Whenever a group's beliefs are challenged it can seek "confirmation" (in a psychological sense only) by convincing others of these beliefs and then, in effect, listening to them. This approach, termed "social validation,"[67] can be used in psychiatry because it is the psychiatrists themselves who hold the power of saying how many mentally ill people there are.[68] Thus Sutherland's study of the diffusion in the 1950's of laws regarding the sexual psychopath depicted a tendency of the psychiatric profession to side with legal authority in the expansion of the realm of social problems, provided psychiatry is given its rightful due.[69] Attempts to psychiatrize criminal justice continue, for example in the dangerous offender proposals of the Canadian Committee on Corrections.[70] The belief that most deviance in society is the product of sick personalities is devoid of scientific support.[71]

Thomas Szasz has offered a far more radical critique of the basis of psychiatric competence by questioning the correctness of the analogy between physical and mental illness.[72] Szasz lays emphasis on the potential to fake the symptoms of mental disorder, on the lack of any independent proof, and on the

---

but many of his views have since been adopted by a veritable army of advocates.

67. For an excellent analysis and example of social validation at work, see Leon Festinger *et al.*, *When Prophecy Fails*, Minneapolis: University of Minnesota Press, 1956.

68. See Richard Hawkins and Gary Tiedeman, *The Creation of Deviance*, Columbus, Ohio: Merrill, 1975, pp. 152-155.

69. Edwin H. Sutherland, "The Diffusion of Sexual Psychopath Laws," *American Journal of Sociology*, 56, 1950, pp. 142-148.

70. See a response in R.R. Price, "Mentally Disordered and Dangerous Persons under the Criminal Law," *Canadian Journal of Corrections*, 12, 1970, pp. 241-264.

71. For a brief overview on this point see Edmund Vaz, *Aspects of Deviance*, Toronto: Prentice-Hall of Canada, 1976, pp. 28-29. For a thorough analysis of the medicalization of deviance see Peter Conrad and Joseph Schneider, *Deviance and Medicalization: From Badness to Sickness*, St. Louis: Mosby, 1980.

72. Thomas S. Szasz, *The Myth of Mental Illness*, New York: Hoeber-Harper, 1961. See also Scheff, *op. cit.*; Merlin Taber *et al.*, "Disease Ideology and Mental Health Research," *Social Problems*, 16, 1969, pp. 349-357.

transference of the prestige of the medical profession into an arena in which cure rates are low.[73] Indeed the very conception of "patients" and "diagnoses" may be *misapplied*.[74] He maintains that he is not anti-psychiatry (he is indeed a more orthodox Freudian than most), but challenges what he sees as the misuse of psychiatry—for instance in forensic psychiatry's expert testimony on the sanity of an accused person.[75] Quite evidently such an accused has every reason to fake the cues of mental illness, and an outcome may depend more on his faking ability (to escape a harsher environment) than on any competence of the psychiatrists to evaluate him.[76]

The same difficulty is present to a lesser extent outside of the courtroom. Szasz correctly notes the advantages that often accrue to one who plays a sick role; the same is true of mental illness except that deception here is harder to penetrate.[77] Some psychiatrists have claimed that a person who fakes mental illness *is* mentally ill by virtue of such a strange action, but surely no such complicated explanation is needed to account for the behaviour of people who stand to gain much from obtaining a verdict of sickness (or think they do).

Szasz at times seems to go one step further than this analysis; he appears to maintain that there is no mental illness at all except that which is organically caused. But there is really no need to take such a radical step in order to recognize the failings

73. More precisely, the verifiable difference between cure rates under treatment and cure rates without it is vanishingly small. See Hans Eysenck, *The Effects of Psychotherapy*, New York: International Science Press, 1966. See also Joseph J. Cocozza and Henry J. Steadman, "Prediction in Psychiatry: An Example of Misplaced Confidence in Experts," *Social Problems*, 23, 1978, pp. 265-276.
74. For excellent discussions of the failings of the medical model of mental "illness," see Scheff, *op. cit.*, and Geoff Baruch and Andrew Treacher, *Psychiatry Observed*, Boston: Routledge, 1978.
75. See Sara Fein and Ken S. Miller, "Legal Process and Adjudication in Mental Incompetency Proceedings," *Social Problems*, 20, 1972, pp. 57-64.
76. It is also ironically true, however, that persons who are adjudged mentally incompetent to stand trial are sometimes kept in mental institutions for longer than the maximum sentence for which they might have been convicted.
77. In effect psychiatrists make decisions on cues "given off" rather than cues "given out" (Erving Goffman, *The Presentation of Self in Everyday Life*, Garden City, New York: Doubleday Anchor, 1959), but such cues are not less amenable to deception than any others.

of psychiatric diagnosis and the widespread unwillingness of the profession to face the reality that symptoms can be faked— the accusers can lie—with all that this implies.[78]

The importance of the defining potential of psychiatry can become quite clear even in the case of persons about whom only an accusation of mental illness has been made; it is more striking still when it is the psychiatric profession itself which first brands a person or group as mentally imbalanced. Unofficial psychiatric diagnosis can be applied by lay persons, groups, or the object of the diagnosis, or indeed any source outside the profession. In fact, this is not infrequently encountered in the conversation of laymen as well as professionals; instant diagnosis of the "disorder" of some other person is endemic in sophisticated circles. It has become something of a conversational game to render quick judgment on the "mental problems" of a mutual acquaintance. But while these lay appraisals may occasionally be consequential for the object of analysis, it is when the psychiatric professionals themselves appraise candidates for political office, whole sectors of the population, occupational groups, or social movements that the power of psychiatric definition becomes most significant.

The potency of this particular labeling act derives from two primary sources. First, by affixing a psychiatric brand to a group or movement, the necessity to answer its arguments may be obviated. Especially if the group is advocating something very different from current practice, the need for counter-argument can be eliminated (in a practical sense) by explaining its actions as symptoms of an underlying mental difficulty— thus youthful, disruptive war-protesters were "Spocked when they should have been spanked." In far more sophisticated language, such major figures of modern psychiatric thought as Bruno Bettelheim have explained away student protest by

---

78. For spirited and informed defenses of the mental illness concept, see David P. Ausubel, "Personality Disorder *Is* Disease," *American Psychologist*, 16, 1961, pp. 69-74; Benjamin Pasamanick, "The Development of Physicians for Public Mental Health," *American Journal of Orthopsychiatry*, 37, 1967, pp. 469-486; J.K. Wing, *Reasoning About Madness,* New York: Oxford University Press, 1978. Contemporary critics of the medical model are legion; they are referenced in Taber *et al., op. cit.*

examining the individual backgrounds of the persons involved rather than their arguments. The same aproach can be taken with respect to arguments of persons on the far political right.

The second source of the power of the psychiatric label lies in the fact that it is not punitive per se. It disarms resistance by pitying rather than condemning, especially when put into the guise of helpful diagnosis. When this is coupled with the expertise of the professional (and the professional's presumed detachment), the defenses usually available against a forthright attack are relatively ineffectual.

There are clear cases of abuse of the profession's labeling power. In 1964, when psychiatrists were respectfully approached by the magazine *Fact* for their opinions of U.S. Presidential candidate Barry Goldwater's mental condition, more than one hundred freely rendered their very negative "professional opinion" of his sanity without ever having seen Goldwater—although, to the credit of the profession, a large number evidently declined to express an opinion or replied that the procedure was incredible. Such branding, with the prestige of psychiatric medicine behind it, has been applied at various times to Hitler, Stalin, the Nazis, the Communists, the police (e.g., sick authoritarians), homosexuals, terrorists, ayatollahs, women's liberation supporters, male chauvinists—in fact, to anyone with whom the labeler does not sympathize. This is not to imply that such categorizing is done deliberately; rather *there is always a tendency to consider positions or actions that we cannot understand as insane or abnormal*, and it is almost always more difficult to understand as rational those positions which we do not agree with than those that we do.[79] To be sure, some persons *are* mentally disturbed. But the appellations of crazy, sick, or insane seem to correspond with distressing regularity to the side of the fence other than that of the labeler.

---

79. In a fine discussion of this form of fuzzy thinking, Elliot Aronson invokes Aronson's first law: "People who do crazy things are not necessarily crazy." See his *The Social Animal*, third edition, San Francisco: Freeman, 1980, p. 8. Aronson goes on to point out that it does not advance things (either our understanding or our defensive effectiveness) to apply psychiatric sickness labels to activities such as terrorism in which a sizable number of persons are involved.

Since most psychiatrists have liberal tendencies, the political right may receive more than an equal share of such treatment, but it can claim no monopoly.

Psychiatric labeling has historically had another important function: to alter the conception of certain deviant behaviours from misconduct to sickness. Inasmuch as the sick are usually treated with greater kindness than miscreants, this amounts to a promotion in terms of public reaction. Two prominent illustrations of this switch have been the re-labeling of alcoholism as a disease instead of a personal weakness, and the recognition of shell shock as distinguishable from military malingering and desertion. However much the role of the sick carries its own disadvantages (see the chapter on differential treatment), in most cases it is more advantageous than the role of the "weak-willed" which it replaces.[80]

IN CONCLUSION: A BRIEF PERSPECTIVE ON INTELLECTUALS' FAILINGS

The negative features of the sections above do not demonstrate a widespread venality among intellectuals and other professionals. These negative aspects are more accurately to be regarded as an inadvertent result of narrow and stereotyped thinking about social problems among the very experts who set out to improve some unattractive aspect of reality. Our criticisms, above, of self-seeking academics, and our critique of the vulnerability of intellectuals in general should not be misconstrued. There is a danger of that, so it should be pointed out that no other collectivity of comparable size brings to bear such a formidable capacity for learning, and such a depth of understanding, on the problems which beset modern society. Many of the criticisms voiced here would apply with even greater strength to other candidates for the role of definer. As Walter Lippmann puts it,

I have not forgotten how often the professors have been proved to be wrong, how often the academic judgment has

80. See Hawkins and Tiedeman, *op. cit.*, p. 250.

been confounded by some solitary thinker or artist, how often original and innovating men have been rejected by the universities, only to be accepted and celebrated after they are dead. The universal company of scholars is not an infallible court of last resort. Far from it. . . . Nevertheless, in the modern world there exists no court which is less fallible than the company of scholars, when we are in the field of truth and error.[81]

The opposite side of the coin to the problems of elitism is what the elitists of the nineteenth century called the "sovereignty of the unqualified." Not long ago critics of mass society were worried that masses in the grip of demagogues could again define Jews or "pinkos" as social problems. We do not argue for a return to the day in which intellectuals were ignored! But neither the intellectuals themselves nor society in general can afford to ignore the systematic tendencies we have touched upon. The intellectuals—for whom the term itself was a derogation not so long ago—may be in danger of assuming too much for themselves in prescribing for society's ills, and others are in danger of endorsing their elitist role.

81. Lippmann, *op. cit.*, p. 17.

7 Stereotype And Ideology As Bases of "Treatment"

We have seen how ideology permeates the entire subject of social problems, starting with which topics are selected for inclusion and how they are regarded. But there is as well another outlet for ideology and stereotype* in this sphere: the differential treatment of persons based on the prevailing (or the powerful) viewpoints concerning causes and cures. In this chapter we will deal with one facet of this phenomenon, *involuntary treatment*: that is, some alteration of a person's condition for "improvements" he or she would rather do without.

After the definition of a social problem has been made, a decision is reached about the nature of a particular person with respect to this problem, and thus a second definition (a label) is affirmed. "The deviant, in short, is made by society in two senses: first, that society makes the rules which he has broken and, secondly, that society 'enforces' them and makes a public declaration announcing that the rules have been broken."[1]

SENTENCING FOR CRIME

The most widely studied form of differential treatment is sentencing for crime. Historically, sentences imposed for crimes were often either wildly idiosyncratic or quite openly based on matters which we would now consider irrelevant—for instance, the offender's status in society. As a result of the writings of

1. Alvin W. Gouldner, "The Sociologist as Partisan: Sociology and the Welfare State," reprinted in *The Sociology of Sociology*, edited by Larry T. Reynolds and Janice M. Reynolds, New York: McKay, 1970, p. 221.

legal and juridical philosophers, the situation was gradually changed. Beccaria, an Italian philosopher-jurist of the eighteenth century, advocated a strictly graduated series of legal sanctions, spelled out clearly in advance, and applied without favour or partiality to everyone convicted of the same offense. Judges were to have no discretion under the system he proposed. Beccaria's writings accomplished many badly needed reforms in the penal practices of the day, but his wisdom on the point noted eventually came under severe criticism: the complete lack of judicial discretion came to be seen as detrimental to another objective which was coming into high regard. Alteration (rehabilitation) of criminals, to allow them to mend their ways when released, became viewed as a critical objective of the penal process, and, according to the reformers, lack of judicial discretion in sentencing was destructive of this end. Judges should be given a certain leeway in sentencing—the newer theory said—so that they could tailor each sentence to the specific needs of the case, in terms of rehabilitation or conversion. There should be recognition of individual differences among the guilty. This latter doctrine of judicial discretion is everywhere triumphant today, so that standard, unalterable sentences are a thing of the past.[2] Judges are provided with boundaries, typically quite broad, for the sentences permissible for a person convicted of a given offense.

But this new way of handling the matter, as well as allowing play for new ideas in penal philosophy, has also brought back the old difficulties of differential treatment. Once again we find persons drawing sentences of varying severity for what are manifestly the same criminal acts. There are several aspects of this problem, not all of which need concern us here. For instance, there is the problem of judges with different overall severity in sentencing,[3] so that a person's sentence depends in part on which judge is drawn. But, above all, what is of concern here is the differential sentencing of offenders on the basis of *personal attributes* that are apparently unrelated either to the

2. This judicial flexibility has been further augmented by flexibility through the mechanism of parole.
3. John Hogarth, *Sentencing as a Human Process*, Toronto: University of Toronto Press, 1971.

crime or to rehabilitation.[4] These attributes include the race of the offender, sex, age, and social class.

The one positive aspect about such discrimination is that it is relatively easy to document. Essentially, one compares sentence lengths (or proportion of sentences suspended) for persons with differing characteristics who commit the same offense. As the sentence of the offense are in each case matters of official record, all that remains is to ascertain the attribute under consideration. In such attributes as sex there is no difficulty here either—the name ordinarily being sufficient.[5]

Such analyses have been done. Men, for instance, are more likely to receive prison sentences than women for a given offense.[6] The most famous study considered the effects of race of the offender. In a survey in the American South, blacks were found to be disproportionately sentenced to prison and given longer terms for the same offenses than were whites.[7] The race of the victim was of marked importance: blacks who victimized whites were treated more harshly than white offenders, but this was not found for blacks who victimized other blacks. Similar analyses have been conducted on other attributes, indicating for instance that young adults (except for adolescents) are more likely to receive stiff sentences than older persons, working-class persons more so than persons from higher socio-economic strata, boys from broken homes more than boys from homes intact. In Florida, where a judge may withhold the label of

4. There is also the problem of perceived public demand (outcry) against certain offenses as a factor in sanctioning severity, and how this may fluctuate over time. See Hogarth, *ibid*.

5. The real offense is sometimes disguised by reductions of the charge which at times accompany pretrial bargaining, though, if anything, this may well *reduce* the evidence of bias.

6. Douglas F. Cousineau and Jean Veevers, "Incarceration as a Response to Crime: The Utilization of Canadian Prisons," *Canadian Journal of Criminology and Corrections*, 14, 1972, pp. 10-36. This is confirmed by the American experience, which also finds women given shorter sentences. See Elmer H. Johnson, *Crime, Correction and Society*, revised edition, Homewood, Ill.: Dorsey Press, 1968.

7. The classic work on effects of race is Henry A. Bullock, "Significance of the Racial Factor in the Lengh of Prison Sentence," *Journal of Criminal Law, Criminology and Police Science*, 52, 1961. See his work elaborated in R.L. McNeely and Carl E. Pope, eds., *Race, Crime, and Criminal Justice*, Beverly Hills, Cal.: Sage, 1981.

convicted if a guilty person is placed on probation, this favour was found more frequently among persons who were white, well educated, without prior record, younger, and defended by a private attorney.[8] Griffiths, Klein, and Verdun-Jones have surveyed the Canadian research on sentencing disparities and biases, reaching similar conclusions.[9]

While the establishment of the patterns is important, interpretation of their meaning is equally essential. The kindest face which can be put on such prejudicial treatment is to speculate that the judges are doing precisely what they were mandated to do—applying sanctions in terms of the perceived "needs" of the offender. It might just happen that judges feel that boys from broken homes are more likely to benefit from custody than are boys from homes with both parents. (Such a conclusion would in itself be of questionable integrity unless some supporting evidence were forthcoming.) But, with the possible exception of the aforementioned boys, it seems very doubtful that judges base their practices on the overt grounds that such criteria as race, sex, age, class are of predictive value in determining the *rehabilitative or preventative worth* of a sentence of a given severity. (For that matter it must be admitted that there is very little information on what judges *do* use as criteria for sentencing.)[10]

Therefore, in order to explain differential treatment based on certain attributes, we must fall back onto less admirable explanations, on covertly held ideas about blacks and whites, males and females, executives and labourers. The vast majority of judges are white, upper middle class (or upper class), old, and male. In all but the last they are themselves in the favoured category in terms of sentencing. Those holding an interest theory of class (read: self-interest or vested interest) may wish to explain this relation on rather obvious grounds. The truth,

---

8. Theodore G. Chiricos *et al.*, "Inequality in the Imposition of a Criminal Label," *Social Problems*, 19, 1972, pp. 553-572.

9. Curt T. Griffiths *et al.*, *Criminal Justice in Canada: An Introductory Text*, Vancouver: Butterworth Western Canada, 1980.

10. See Hogarth, *op. cit.*, and Edward Green, *Judicial Attitudes in Sentencing*, London: Macmillan, 1961.

however, seems to be that the judges are themselves largely unaware of these trends, and feel that they examine each case on its own merits. Their behaviour might be better regarded as exemplifying their stereotype respecting the kind of person they are dealing with.

Certainly judges see before them many more men than women, workers than executives, younger adults than old, and—either in proportion to their ratios in the total population or even in absolute numbers—more blacks and Indians than whites. And this may in turn lead them to draw certain conclusions about these attributes.[11] When an atypical offender appears before a judge (as, ideally, an old, white, upper-class lady—already we say "lady") the tendency is to perceive such a person as basically non-criminal, reformable. When a young, unemployed, Indian or black male appears, however, exactly the opposite is likely to occur. It is not so much that the judge consciously reflects upon the person's attributes but that the attributes provide cues which trigger a particular frame of mind. As the psychologists might say, the judge is perceptually ready to see certain qualities, good or bad, in the person.[12]

What is true of judges must also occur with juries, although in subtly different ways. A jury member, of course, is not typically upper middle class and old. The juror's perceptual biases may be altogether different from those of the judge, and there may be a difference in the readiness to appraise the defendant on the basis of specific attributes. But juries too have their preconceptions; for jurisdictions in which the juries, rather than the judge, pass sentence, there are also differentials in sentence based on attribute rather than offense. It is for this reason that court decisions requiring women and blacks to be eligible jurors, in numbers proportionate to their frequency in the population, are so potentially significant.

11. There are biases already at work in these differences, but we reserve this discussion for later.
12. Jerome S. Bruner, "On Perceptual Readiness," in *Current Perspectives in Social Psychology*, edited by E.P. Hollander and Raymond G. Hunt, New York: Oxford University Press, 1963, pp. 42-47.

THE DECISION TO ARREST

We have discussed judicial discretion as a source of preferential treatment, but there is another covert process in the criminal justice system which must be examined here. As has often been noted, it is manifestly impossible for a legislature to set down rules for law enforcement officials which can cover the infinity of discrete situations encountered in practice. Many occasions exist in which a policeman must use his own judgment in deciding whether or not to make an arrest.[13] This is most typically the case for relatively minor or marginal offenses, in which the statutory language is intentionally vague. In contrast to the relative precision with which such a serious crime as rape is defined, laws regarding loitering, disturbing the peace, public nuisance, drunk and disorderly conduct, or interference with a peace officer on official duty are necessarily less specific, having to cover a broad range of concrete instances in multi-dimensional situations. For such offenses, what is termed *police discretion* is quite apparent. The officer must decide whether the person should be ignored, lectured, sent home in a taxi, remanded to parents, or arrested. The officer on the spot must be allowed considerable latitude because of the heterogeneity of situations in which a given law may apply.[14]

Difficulties therefore arise and minor offenses are frequently handled in a discriminatory way. No one doubts that police arrest murderers in a systematic fashion, but what of drunks? The man drunk in his Cadillac in a fashionable section of town is guided to a taxi; the grizzled old man on skid row is arrested and hustled into the drunk tank because it is assumed that he does not have a home. Nor need we depend on casual observa-

13. Police discretion is also unavoidable in deciding which calls to police headquarters are worth responding to. See Brian Grosman, "The Discretionary Enforcement of Law," *Chitty's Law Journal*, 21, 1973.

14. See Brian Grosman, *Police Command: Decisions and Discretion*, Agincourt, Ontario: Macmillan of Canada, 1975. "It is significant, however, that in spite of the fact that such marginal offenses consume the bulk of their time, law enforcement personnel typically receive little or no training in handling them." The President's Commission on Law Enforcement and Administration of Justice, *The Challenge of Crime in a Free Society*, Washington, D.C.: U.S. Government Printing Office, 1967, pp. 91-92, 106-113.

tion to confirm this trend: observers have accompanied police on their rounds and systematically recorded bias in the decision to arrest.[15] Much the same factors come into play with police discretion as with judicial and jury discretion—old, white, female, and middle or upper class persons are less likely to be taken into custody for the same offense.[16] The evidence for discretionary bias against Indians with respect to minor or marginal offenses is overwhelming.[17]

Let us put some detail into this general picture. In an elegant little study in California, Heussenstamm asked a group of fifteen student volunteers to display prominent Black Panther bumper stickers on their cars at the height of scares about black power. Although none of the students in the group had received a single moving traffic violation in the preceding twelve months, without any conscious change in driving habits they quickly amassed a total of 33 traffic citations from police in a seventeen day period, at which point the study was prematurely halted.[18] This study nicely demonstrates the point that police discretion can be abused not only on the basis of *personal attributes* (race, age, sex, etc.) but also on the basis of one's *political affiliations.* Additional factors are also at work:[19] the locale of apprehension, the time of day, whether the officer thinks a conviction will "stick" and, most importantly, the *demeanour* of the suspect.[20]

15. The most extensive study is Wayne R. LaFave's *Arrest: The Decision to Take a Suspect into Custody*, Boston: Little, Brown, 1964.
16. For explicit detailed confirmation of these biases with respect to marijuana arrests versus marijuana use, see Weldon T. Johnson *et al.,* "Arrest Probabilities for Marijuana Users as Indicators of Selective Law Enforcement," *American Journal of Sociology,* 83, 1977, pp. 681-700.
17. See the evidence in Rita Bienvenue and A.H. Latif, "Arrests, Dispositions and Recidivism: A Comparison of Indians and Whites," *Canadian Journal of Criminology and Corrections,* 16, 1974, pp. 105-116, as well as the other studies they cite.
18. F.K. Heussenstamm, "Bumper Stickers and the Cops," in *Contemporary Social Psychology: Representative Readings,* edited by Thomas Blass, Itasca, Ill.: Peacock, 1976, pp. 137-140.
19. LaFave, *op. cit.*
20. For an excellent overview of police discretion in both Canada and the U.S., ethical and practical arguments, and a review of the recent literature on the effects of the police department environment, the characteristics of the offender, and the arrest situation, see Griffiths, *op. cit.,* pp. 97-115.

TREATMENT BY POLICE

There is another aspect of differential treatment that takes place even without arrest: the demeanour of the police—their verbal aggressiveness, gentleness or roughness in handling a person. This difference in treatment is dependent in large part upon the factors and personal attributes discussed above, but especially on the behaviour of the subject at the time of confrontation. Is he arrogant, or uncooperative? Police admit privately to the difficulty of the arrest setting and to their own apprehensiveness. At times they must walk into extremely dangerous situations and defuse them solely by their "front."[21] They develop the feeling that it is vital to obtain quick command of any encounter, and a distinctive manner is developed to promote this. An ability to evaluate a situation rapidly is also prized, and this of course requires observance of outwardly visible cues such as race, age, and sex. The front displayed in a given situation is adjusted accordingly.[22] But while one can be sympathetic with such a difficult task, the picture from the standpoint of the suspect is quite different, for if he happens to be displaying the wrong cues he is immediately subjected to an aggressive, overbearing hostility, which evokes the most extreme emotions. It is this verbal aggressiveness to which blacks often refer when speaking of police brutality. The scene often degenerates into a status game in which the policeman, to attain the security which comes with dominance, places greater and greater requirements on the individual (e.g., demands for identification, a frisk search), while to maintain his own feeling of self-worth the suspect performs all required actions with greater and greater disdain and arrogance. Eventually he may feel internally compelled to disobey an order or to verbally

21. This requirement helps explain why police officers back one another to the hilt in investigations of impropriety.
22. For research on the evaluation of suspects by policemen see Irving Piliavin and Scott Briar, "Police Encounters with Juveniles," *American Journal of Sociology,* 70, 1964, pp. 206-214; Richard J. Lundman *et al.,* "Police Control of Juveniles: A Replication," *Journal of Research in Crime and Delinquency,* 15, January, 1978; John M. Gandy, "The Exercise of Discretion by the Police as a Decision-Making Process in the Disposition of Juvenile Offenders," *Osgoode Hall Law Journal,* 8, 1970, pp. 333-346.

insult the officer, which may lead to an arrest arising purely from the confrontation.

Even in the absence of an arrest, it is clear that law officers' stereotypes of the public result in differential treatment, sometimes in an extreme form. Inasmuch as their perception of an individual leads to actions on their part which may result in the subjects becoming violent or abusive, it may be said that the police often engage in a self-fulfilling prophecy.*[23] In fairness, it must be added that certain members of the public also have preconceptions of the police, which lead *them* to perform actions in the encounter which drive the police to more drastic steps.

Stereotyping of the suspect occurs at every stage in the criminal justice process—at the initial encounter, the decision to arrest, the arrival at the verdict, and the severity of the sentence.[24] (It is probably at work, too, in parole decisions.) We have discussed some of the self-fulfilling effects of such stereotyping when we looked at labeling or reaction theory, so for now it is sufficient to note two points. First is the fact that popular stereotypes, or in some cases, ideologies, result in preferential treatment having nothing to do with the offense and little if anything to do with rehabilitation potential or "individualized" treatment. Second, official statistics on the characteristics of offenders (for example, the proportion of convicts who are blacks, or men, or juveniles) are distorted by these mechanisms, so that some categories will be over-

23. See in this connection Kelly G. Shaver, "Interpersonal and Social Consequences of Attribution," in *Contemporary Issues in Social Psychology*, Third Edition, edited by J.L. Brigham and L.S. Wrightsman, Monterey, Cal.: Brooks, Cole, 1977, especially pp. 323-325; John P. Clark, "Isolation of the Police: A Comparison of British and American Situations," *Journal of Criminal Law, Criminology, and Police Science*, 56, 1965, pp. 307-319. For an elaboration of such points (and their limitations) in Canada see Daniel J. Koenig, "Police Perceptions of Public Respect and Extra-Legal Use of Force," *Canadian Journal of Sociology*, 1, 1975, pp. 313-324.
24. Stereotyping also takes place with respect to the victim of crime, so that in some jurisdictions officials respond with leniency toward the offender when the victim is a minority group member—the so-called "indulgent pattern" of enforcement—and with greater harshness when the victim is not (the "nonindulgent pattern"). See Bullock, *op. cit.*

represented—perhaps markedly so.[25] *Insofar as such statistics form the basis for selective enforcement, they are to that extent self-fulfilling.* As one example, if blacks are over-represented, and law officers are more or less aware of the statistics, they will be watching blacks more closely, will be more likely to apprehend a black criminal than a white, and they may trigger more illegal reactions with blacks than with whites. As more blacks are brought in, the perception of criminality among blacks becomes self-confirming.[26]

SELECTING THE MENTALLY ILL

The term "treatment" in the title of this chapter may fit most closely the condition known as mental illness, and we find here the questions of ideology and perception at least as strong as in the treatment of the accused criminal. The issues involving the definition of mental abnormality and the attachment of medical labels to what may be just problems of living have been covered in the previous chapter. We are not concerned here with the validity of the illness analogy, but with the power dimension in the involuntary commitment of individuals. Here once again an ideological component is dominant, and once again the name of Thomas Szasz is pre-eminent. As before, when he virtually denied the existence of psychopathology (except as imposed by labeling), Szasz at points allows himself to be carried away in his argument. But the facts he presents regarding the misuse of psychiatry in legal commitment are too strong to be overcome by his failings.[27]

---

25. There are many mechanisms besides stereotype which lead to the statistical over-representation of certain groups. Financial inequalities lead to differences in the competence of attorneys and the feasibility of appeals. Court procedures may be totally baffling to uneducated defendants. The court language may be unintelligible, for instance to Puerto Ricans in New York City or Eskimos in the Canadian Northwest.
26. See Aaron V. Cicourel, *The Social Organization of Juvenile Justice*, New York: Wiley, 1968; Richard L. Henshel, "Effects of Disciplinary Prestige on Predictive Accuracy: Distortions from Feedback," *Futures*, 7, 1975, pp. 92-106.
27. On a related point, see Henry J. Steadman, "The Psychiatrist as a Conservative Agent of Social Control," *Social Problems*, 20, 1972, pp. 263-271.

As previously mentioned, Szasz argues that mental illness is essentially different from physical illness and that people defined as mentally ill are not sick at all but have in fact problems of living.[28] They sometimes make a nuisance of themselves, and may be unhappy, but in contrast to a physical illness in which the afflicted one is almost always among the first to complain, such persons often will not concede their need for any help. At the very least, one must agree with Szasz that a diagnosis of mental ill-health cannot be made with the exactitude one expects in the case of a broken leg or a ruptured appendix.[29] If so, then there is much more room for bias in the decision—all the more so since the "patient" often does not concur.

Yet Szasz has documented the extremely slipshod, hurried, and careless ways in which people are often examined in order to affix a label which will be of the utmost consequence for the rest of their lives.[30] Not only are the procedures incredibly bad, but the legal safeguards designed to catch such errors in labeling in ordinary legal trials are almost totally lacking for decisions involving involuntary commitment to mental institutions.

To understand why this is the case it is necessary to penetrate the doctrinal foundations of involuntary commitment. Involuntary commitment is for the patient's own good; psychiatry is related to the subject in a helping rather than a punitive role. Hence, this argument goes, a person does not need the safeguards in a commitment proceeding as in a criminal trial—technically it is a civil rather than a criminal case unless a crime has been committed. Since no one is against him—he is not charged with anything—he needs no protection; it is not an

28. Thomas Szasz, *The Myth of Mental Illness*, New York: Hoeber-Harper, 1961. It is interesting to mention that certain mental hospitals are now called "Institutes of Living." See Steve Pratt and Jay Tooley, "Innovations in Mental Hospital Concepts and Practice," in *Major American Social Problems*, by Robert A. Dentler, Chicago: Rand McNally, 1967.
29. This is also expressed in E. Erikson, "The Nature of Clinical Evidence," in *Evidence and Inference*, edited by Daniel Lerner, Glencoe, Ill.: Free Press, 1959, pp. 73-95.
30. See especially Part I of his *Psychiatric Justice*, New York: Basic Books, 1966, and Luis Kutner, "The Illusion of Due Process in Commitment Proceedings," *Northwestern Law Review*, 57, 1962, pp. 383-399.

adversary system. This is the official doctrinal basis of such events, supported both by the traditional divisions of the law and by the self-conception of the psychiatric profession that it is a healing, helping, certainly non-punitive endeavour.[31]

As a result of these views, the traditional trappings of criminal justice have been dispensed with, most importantly those safeguarding an accused against erroneous findings. With only minor variations between different jurisdictions, persons at psychiatric examinations generally have no privilege against self-incrimination, no right to remain silent, no right to be informed of the claims made against them, nor who made them (and often are not so informed), no right to summon witnesses on their behalf, nor to compel their testimony, nor to cross-examine, nor to be represented by counsel. They are frequently not advised of their right to challenge the proceedings or of their later right to seek release. In most instances, no lawyer may speak for them and no psychiatrist may represent their interests or even—in most cases—translate the psychiatric findings into lay terms.

This procedure is justified on the ground that it is for the benefit of the patients themselves, as in conventional medicine, but the facts do not always appear to bear this out. In the first place, the essence of involuntary commitment is that the person does not wish to go. At the very onset, then, we experience a conflict of values which is only rarely found in the medical model.[32] But even under a sort of involuntary humanitarianism, the case for such legal procedures is poor. Mental institutions are terribly over-crowded, their staffs inadequate, and their deprivations severe.

In some cases, the review process for persons once admitted to the institution is deficient and even where it is satisfactory in the formal sense there is an additional problem. Rosenhan arranged to have a number of willing volunteer graduate students committed by court order to twelve different mental hospitals, in order to conduct an experiment on how readily the

31. See Nicholas Kittrie, *The Right to be Different*, Baltimore: Johns Hopkins University Press, 1971.
32. Certain religious groups object to vaccination; suicide prevention also exhibits certain ethical similarities.

hospital psychiatric staffs would recognize their sanity. Beyond their initial commitment reason (that they heard voices), the students were instructed to behave perfectly naturally, and answer all questions truthfully. Not only did no psychiatric staff member in any hospital recognize the difference even once, but the students experienced great difficulty in getting out at the appropriate time. This result has been interpreted to show that once a diagnosis is made on a person it *sticks* to him—as Rosenhan put it "the normal are not detectably sane"—especially not inside an institution.[33] Not inaccurately, Szasz compares psychiatric hearings to trials in which a life sentence may result. When it is recognized that in the United States close to a quarter of a million persons are involuntarily committed every year, the magnitude of the situation is clear. In most areas, the proportion of commitments which are involuntary is very high. In Canada, 83% of the commitments in 1960 were of this nature.[34] Moreover, in the United States, it has been found that persons from the lower classes are more likely to be involuntarily committed,[35] and this is particularly true of blacks.[36] The incorrectness of ignoring the inadvertent punitive aspects of such confinement is obvious.[37]

Szasz advances beyond the indisputable charge that important and well-nigh irreversible decisions about people's lives are being made in unconscionably cavalier fashion. He also feels that, while psychiatry is always helpful in theory, in

33. D.L. Rosenhan, "On being Sane in Insane Places," *Science*, 179, 1973, pp. 250-258. See also Richard Hawkins and Gary Tiedeman, *The Creation of Deviance*, Columbus, Ohio: Merrill, 1975, p. 198.

34. See Alex Richman, *Psychiatric Care in Canada: Extent and Results*, Royal Commission on Health Services, Ottawa: Queen's Printer, 1966, p. 70.

35. W.A. Rushing, "Status Resources, Societal Reactions, and Hospital Admission," *American Sociological Review*, 43, 1978, pp. 521-533.

36. B.A. Baldwin *et al.*, "Status Inconsistency and Psychiatric Diagnoses: A Structural Approach to Labeling Theory," *Journal of Health and Social Behavior*, 16, 1975, pp. 257-267.

37. The argument that a legal decision is non-punitive because it does not formally involve criminal sanctions is not a new one. The House Un-American Activities Committee in the United States used to justify its persecution of "communists," "pinkos," and others by the same argument: since it could not fine, imprison or execute, it had no real sanctioning power and hence did not require the safeguards of a criminal court. Those who felt the effects of its blacklisting practices may not have felt so sanguine about its power to punish.

practice it is sometimes serving its own interests, at least with respect to involuntary therapy, which Szasz sees as a contradiction in terms. Even in the absence of commitment to an institution, the label "mental illness" is a socially disabling one—however well intended.[38] It is therefore anathema to Szasz to regard whatever the psychiatrist does as being necessarily in the best interest of the patient. It is precisely *because* the mental illness label is not hostile or punitive per se that it is so insidious in its ability to weaken the defenses of the person who is being helped. A person so charged is more vulnerable, more directly accessible to public agencies or individuals who do not always have his or her best interests at heart.[39] This is one of Szasz's chief points in *The Ethics of Psychoanalysis*.[40]

A realistic view of commitment decisions is one which takes account of the power and conflict involved. By defining people as sick and in need of hospitalization, they can be gotten out of the way and "taken care of" even though they have done nothing illegal and have merely made nuisances of themselves.[41] As such, decisions go far beyond the psychiatrist's healing role and involve him in non-scientific tasks as an agent of social control.[42] As Szasz points out, people "put away" other people partly because they do not want them around. The individuals

38. Hawkins and Tiedeman, *op. cit.* The "Eagleton affair" in the 1972 American Presidential election, in which Eagleton—an otherwise excellent candidate— was dropped because of an earlier bout of mental disability years before, is a case in point.

39. Although we have thus far concentrated on involuntary commitment, it is clear that such power extends beyond the walls of the asylum into the lives of persons judged sane enough to manage outside but supposedly not well enough to make an autonomous appraisal of their own mental state.

40. Thomas S. Szasz, *The Ethics of Psychoanalysis*, New York: Basic Books, 1965.

41. There is something of a parallel between this situation and the enforcement of loitering and vagrancy laws. See Richard Quinney, *The Social Reality of Crime*, Boston: Little, Brown, 1970.

42. In the past decade, the psychiatric profession has come under attack for acting as an agent of social control with respect to "appropriate" femininity. See, for instance, Phyllis Chesler, "Patient and Patriarch: Women in the Psychotherapeutic Relationship," in *Women in Sexist Society*, edited by Vivian Gornick and Barbara K. Moran, New York: Basic Books, 1971, and in her *Women and Madness*, New York: Avon, 1972.

involved in the decision-making process—petitioners (usually relatives), psychiatrists, and court officials—all have certain vested interests in the outcome which they seek to promote. At times these are the easy to understand motivations of disenchanted spouses or relatives, but at other times it may be officialdom itself which is the prime mover in the process. Szasz forcefully condemns the misuse of psychiatry to cover administrative actions. He cites instances in which officials have had bothersome persons committed. Especially iniquitous is the practice of declaring someone incompetent to stand trial. This was originally intended as a protection but, as it has developed, a person may be incarcerated through it in a mental hospital for longer than the corresponding maximum sentence could have been, and without the need of the prosecution to prove his or her criminal guilt.[43]

Some of Szasz's arguments appear excessive. In his zeal to divorce psychiatry completely from the legal machinery, he would rule out entirely the insanity plea in criminal trials, even if the accused prefers it. He seems to feel that involuntary hospitalization never does any good to the patient, and, in describing self-serving machinations, he completely overlooks altruistic motives in psychiatrists. It is true that many psychiatrists gain from forensic work and that the profession needs patients to validate its occupational role, but these features are considerably exaggerated in Szasz's analysis.[44] In spite of such defects, Szasz has performed a significant service in bringing glaring inequities to the public eye.[45]

---

43. See Barry Swadron, "The Unfairness of Unfitness," *Canadian Bar Review*, 9, 1966, pp. 76-77 and 113; Mark E. Schiffer, "Fitness to Stand Trial," *University of Toronto Faculty of Law Review*, 35, 1977, pp. 1-25. The American situation is equivalent.
44. See a more accurate portrayal in Chapter 6 of Hawkins and Tiedeman, *op. cit.*, "Controlling Deviance is Big Business."
45. However, there is by no means a consensus on this point among psychiatrists. See Arlene Kaplan Daniels, "Professional Responses to 'Insider' Critics: Psychiatrists Consider Dr. Szasz," paper presented at the annual meeting of the Society for the Study of Social Problems, New Orleans, 1972.

SOCIAL CLASS AND TREATMENT OF MENTAL ILLNESS

In the 1950's Hollingshead and Redlich published a landmark study on social class and mental illness.[46] In view of the idea that selection and treatment of a social problem tend to proceed along stereotypical lines, their findings are of considerable interest.

In their study of a New England community, Hollingshead and Redlich first examined the type of diagnosis for mental illness that members of different social classes received. First, they found that lower-class individuals were over-represented among people who were mental patients or were being treated for mental illness:[47] While persons in class V (the lower-lower class in that particular study) constituted 38% of all patients, class V people constituted only 18% of the total non-patient population.[48] Furthermore, when *types* of disorders were taken into consideration, and globally subdivided into neuroses and psychoses, only about 19% of the class V patients had been diagnosed as neurotic while some 65% of class I patients had been so labeled.[49] Neuroses are usually considered milder problems and are less subject to stigma; it is thus interesting to note that so few lower-class patients had received such a diagnosis.

Ignoring the possibility of very large and systematic errors in diagnosis, these disparities are traceable to two possible causes. Either the life styles and experiences of the various social classes were so different that they exerted a strong influence on the type of mental disorder that arose, or, since psychiatric diagnosis depends upon observation of the verbal and non-verbal acts of the subjects, the social class backgrounds of different persons showed up in their behaviour, and these behavioural differences led to systematic differences in

46. August B. Hollingshead and Frederick C. Redlich, *Social Class and Mental Illness*, New York: Wiley, 1958.
47. *Ibid.*, p. 199.
48. *Ibid.*
49. *Ibid.*, p. 223. Similar findings have been reported in other studies. See, for instance, Leo Srole et al., *Mental Health in the Metropolis: The Midtown Manhattan Study*, New York: McGraw-Hill, 1962.

the diagnosis.[50] On the one hand the first hypothesis is supported by certain facts for, indeed, lower-class persons are subjected to more stressful and insecure life conditions,[51] while at the same time receiving fewer of the rewards that higher-status persons receive.[52] Such a negative imbalance may give rise to more serious emotional problems. Moreover, there is evidence that the socialization pattern of lower-class persons often equips them less adequately to cope with stress than does the socialization of persons of higher status.[53] The two explanations are not mutually exclusive, and the second possibility is supported indirectly by the type of treatment that members of different classes received.

In the Hollingshead and Redlich study, treatment was divided for purposes of analysis into three categories: psychotherapy, organic therapy (insulin, electroshock, tranquillizers), and custodial care (which rests on the assumption that little can be done for a mental patient beyond providing him with a shelter).[54] It should be noted that neurotics usually receive psychotherapy while psychotics tend to be given custodial care and organic therapy. Since, as we saw, a greater proportion of lower-class patients had received a psychotic label, proportionately more lower-class patients were subjected to more drastic methods of treatment (e.g., electroshock). But, *even within the same diagnosed condition* there were marked disparities in the frequencies with which patients from various classes received these three types of therapy. Neurotic patients from the lower class, for example, received far more custodial

50. The disparity in the proportion of neurotics may also reflect the fact that upper-class neurotics voluntarily appear for treatment proportionally more often than is the case for working-class individuals. The latter are more frequently referred by social agencies and the courts (or the police) after their behaviour has drawn attention upon them and been considered anti-social.

51. T.S. Langner and S.T. Michael, *Life Stress and Mental Health*, Glencoe, Ill.: Free Press, 1963; R. Liem and J. Liem, "Social Class and Mental Illness Reconsidered: The Role of Economic Stress and Social Support," *Journal of Health and Social Behavior*, 1978, 19, pp. 139-156.

52. Liem and Liem, *ibid*; N. Bradburn, *The Structure of Psychological Well-being*, Chicago: Aldine, 1969.

53. R.C. Kessler and P.D. Cleary, "Social Class and Psychological Distress, *American Journal of Sociology*, 45, 1980, pp. 463-478.

54. Hollingshead and Redlich, op. cit., p. 257.

care than did patients from other classes.[55] And, even when they received psychotherapy, it was of the type called directive, whereas upper-class patients received analytic therapy far more frequently.[56]

Among those neurotics who received psychotherapy, lower-class patients were seen by their practitioners for far fewer visits than upper-class patients,[57] and the length of each session was dismally short for lower-class neurotics.[58] And other investigators on the team also found that "patient's class status determines the professional level of the therapist who treats him."[59]

Of course, certain of these treatment differentials are related to the lower income of class V patients, to their inability to secure expensive treatment. However, Hollingshead and Red-lich found factors other than income to account for this differential. For instance, in public hospitals where treatment is free for all classes, lower-class neurotics still received more custodial care than other classes, and *no* class I neurotic received such a treatment.[60]

Finally, the lengths of time in treatment for each disorder were strikingly different for the several social classes, with psychotics manifesting the greatest social class differences. In classes I and II (higher class), 50% of the patients had been in treatment for less than three years, while in class V, 50% of the patients had been in treatment for ten years.[61]

In sum, then, social class was of considerable significance in its relationship to the disorder diagnosed, the type of treatment received by those with a given disorder, and the length of treatment. Hollingshead and Redlich were not content to set

55. *Ibid.*, p. 267.
56. *Ibid.*, p. 268.
57. *Ibid.*, p. 369.
58. *Ibid.*, p. 270.
59. Jerome K. Myers and Leslie Schaffer, "Social Stratification and Psychiatric Practice," *American Sociological Review*, 19, 1954, pp. 307-310.
60. Hollingshead and Redlich, *op. cit.*, p. 274.
61. *Ibid.*, p. 298. Part of this discrepancy may be accounted for by the greater proportion of schizophrenics among class V patients, but it is probably due more to the greater use of custodial care as the sole "treatment" of class V individuals—including hospitalized neurotics.

forth these facts as simple data; they searched for the meaning behind them. *Why* were these facts found?

The authors rejected the idea that these treatment differentials were entirely due to biases on the part of psychiatrists and staff. Broadly speaking, successful psychotherapy requires a cooperative attitude on the part of the subject. Investigators encountered considerable hostility directed toward the psychiatric profession from lower-class patients, as well as from their families. In addition, few individuals from classes IV or V could understand interpersonal interaction as a means of therapy. Even after long periods of time, many hoped that after "all the talking" they would get down to "treatment." The hostility toward the psychiatrist and the lack of comprehension of verbal therapy clearly diminished the likelihood of progress in those individuals who could have benefited. The investigators also encountered attitudes of rejection among lower-class families toward the member who had been placed under treatment. In most of these cases, psychological support dropped sharply, and the individual's subsequent chances of being cared for at home were very low. Continued hospitalization was seen as preferable in such instances, and undoubtedly this impacted on the statistics on length of treatment cited earlier.

After all of this is mentioned, however, it becomes clear that such factors are insufficient to account for the findings on length of treatment, and totally inadequate with regard to type and quality of treatment. Instead, the attitudes of psychiatrists toward patients must undergo examination. Hollingshead and Redlich investigated the attitudes of the psychiatrists in their study along three major dimensions. They tried to assess whether "(a) those psychiatrists held similar views toward life and society with their patients, (b) they noticed differences in social class between themselves and their patients, and (c) they liked their patients."[62] In general, class I through III patients were liked and class IV and V patients disliked. This is not surprising since most psychiatrists come from class I and II backgrounds. Values and views toward life held by psychia-

62. *Ibid.*, p. 344.

trists and class IV and V patients were markedly dissimilar, and these differences were definitely recognized by the psychiatrists. In effect the psychiatrist and lower-class patient had little to say to one another, and they experienced grave communication difficulties. The psychiatrists were irritated by the lower-class patients' inability to think in their terms— partially a result of vast differences in formal education.

With these factors in mind, the treatment differentials become understandable, if not necessarily excusable. Contemporary psychiatry seems most feasible when communication between patient and therapist is relatively smooth. When this is not the case, the temptation is to turn the problem over to organic therapy or to relegate the patient to custodial care. All too often such decisions follow class lines for the reasons discussed above. But such reasoning does not explain why it is the least skilled and least experienced therapists who are assigned lower-class patients: if they are the hardest to reach and yet psychotherapy is attempted, it makes more sense to use one's most skillful psychiatrists.[63] The only explanation is that such work is "beneath" the more prestigious therapist, who treats whom he wants, and wants to treat those he can get along with. But the authors present a more telling criticism when they point out that "it is not the patient's job to understand the psychiatrist, but it is the psychiatrist's job to understand the patient ... The psychiatrist should not overlook the social differences between himself and his patients, but he should understand them, face them squarely, and deal with them in the therapeutic situation."[64] Until this takes place to a significant degree, differential treatment on a class basis will continue, justified by labels which put the onus on the lower-class patient. Again, we find cultural and stereotypical factors at work in the treatment of a social problem.

IDEOLOGY AND SELECTION OF "MENTALLY ILL" DEVIANTS

At this point we shift our attention with respect to involuntary psychiatric treatment from perceptual and stereotypic matters

63. *Ibid.*, pp. 348-349.
64. *Ibid.*, p. 346.

to concerns pertaining clearly to conscious ideology. Admittedly this distinction is sometimes less than clear-cut, but often the degree to which an ideology, as an overt and organized system of thought, intrudes into the selection process is easily recognizable. We begin, as the title indicates, with ideology in the selection of mentally ill deviants. Szasz has documented cases of ideologically based selection with considerable care.

One item which came to public view in the early 1960's, and which illustrates an ideological component in involuntary commitment, was the case of General Edwin Walker, a right-winger so extreme that he was forced to retire from the United States Army. At the time of the enforced enrollment of the first black at the University of Mississippi in 1962, Walker was at the scene as an outspoken supporter of the segregationist rioters. His exact role is in dispute but, while under arrest for various federal charges, he was suddenly whisked away by plane before bail bond could be posed. He was taken from Mississippi to a federal hospital in Springfield, Missouri, to undergo psychiatric examination. Already there was an affidavit waiting which affirmed "sensitivity and essentially unpredictable and seemingly bizarre outbursts of the type often observed in paranoid individuals," said affidavit having been made by a government psychiatrist who had never seen Walker but relied upon news clippings and his past testimony before a committee of Congress. Because of the publicity the case generated and his public prominence, Walker was able to obtain release from the hospital, choose his own psychiatrist, and, eventually, obtain a ruling of sanity. Lesser persons in such ideological encounters may not fare so well. It is disturbingly evident that psychiatry was used in this case to get rid of Walker because of his views. Szasz also discusses the insanity case of the celebrated poet, Ezra Pound. Although the views of Pound and Walker were far apart, their cases were in certain respects very similar.[65]

The Soviet Union has had a long history of the use of the insane asylum for political purposes, dating back to the incarceration of writers by the *Okhraina*, the secret police of the tsars. These "sane asylums" were immortalized by Chekhov's

---

65. Thomas S. Szasz, *Law, Liberty and Psychiatry*, New York: Macmillan, 1963.

Ward 6, and, more recently, publication of Valery Tarsis's *Ward 7* has confirmed the continued refinement of the practice by Soviet authorities.[66] Tarsis, acclaimed outside of the USSR as a brilliant writer, was himself committed to a Soviet institution after publication of an earlier work. His autobiographical novel portrays an institution in which the inmates are quite sane and the hospital staff is more or less aware that it is a branch of the political police. In such a situation we have a highly refined ideological basis of "treatment" of what is evidently taken to be social problem—in this case, unrepentant, unpatriotic writers.[67]

THE IDEOLOGICAL BASIS IN NON-WESTERN CULTURES

As we have previously pointed out, analysis of social problems is often confined to Western societies. Yet any sophisticated analytical treatment must examine non-Western categories of problems as well. A full adherence to this approach would be so novel vis-a-vis contemporary, parochial discussions that it would demand book-length treatment in itself.[68] We cannot hope to analyze the treatment of non-Western categories of social problems in detail here, but a brief exploration of one particular historical approach is nonetheless instructive in our survey of ideology and treatment. We will take up the efforts in the Peoples Republic of China to deal with the survival of "bourgeois tendencies" after the abolition of capitalism, as this is viewed in China. This is instructive from the standpoint of ideology and treatment since we can easily see conflicting notions of what the problem and the solutions are. From our Western standpoint the employment of inhumane measures to

---

66. Valery Tarsis, *Ward 7*, New York: Dutton, 1965.
67. For extensive coverage, details, and documentation of this problem see Amnesty International's report, *Prisoners of Conscience in the USSR: Their Treatment and Conditions*, second edition, London: Amnesty International Publications, 1980.
68. See S.N. Eisenstadt, ed., *Comparative Social Problems*, New York: Free Press, 1964, for a first approximation to this objective. It compares social problems around the world but the categories are those of Western social science. See Vytautas Kavolis, *Comparative Perspectives on Social Problems*, Boston: Little, Brown, 1969, for an attempt to find an objective basis for a cross-cultural study of social problems.

change people's beliefs constitutes a social problem in itself. From the standpoint of the Chinese cadre in charge of programmes, these same measures were solutions. Inasmuch as bourgeois tendencies, "evil remnants" and "ideological poisons" tend to be ideologically defined, we would expect "treatment" for these matters to also be placed on a doctrinal, ideological basis. We will adhere closely in the following to Robert Jay Lifton's thorough examination of the historical period in China in his *Thought Reform and the Psychology of Totalism*.[69] Later, we will note the psycho-social correspondences between the treatment there and a treatment programme for delinquency that has been much debated and discussed in the United States.

The Communist Revolution in China was an intensely moral affair, and although re-education proceeded slowly at first, it eventually permeated every aspect of Chinese cultural life. In certain periods it was not sufficient for a person to remain neutral or unconcerned about politics: one had to be whole-heartedly committed to the new system and the orthodox ideology, and eventually one had to display one's enthusiasm openly and fervently. Certain categories of persons were especially suspect in the new China, essentially those "classes" who had fared relatively well before the Revolution, and those individuals most critically suspect were systematically subjected to intensive treatment designed to convert them. Such was the experience accorded Westerners in general who remained in China as well as Chinese intellectuals who had received their education in the West.[70] The former were arrested and underwent brainwashing in prisons; the latter were induced and coerced into "volunteering" for re-education. But while the outward manifestations differed for these two types, the intent, the doctrinal basis, and the psycho-social mechanisms of their treatment were highly similar.

---

69. Robert Jay Lifton, *Thought Reform and the Psychology of Totalism*, New York: Norton, 1969. Since the Great Proletarian Cultural Revolution of 1966, and even perhaps before, Lifton's work has become severely dated in certain important aspects. However, as an example in our survey of the ideological basis of treatment, this difficulty is not especially significant, for we make no effort to be "topical" on what is really a generic aspect of social problems.
70. Paradoxically, many of the most important Chinese communists themselves had Western (typically Parisian) educations.

The medical treatment analogy is well taken, here, for there can be little doubt—either from the nature of the experiences undergone or the official doctrine itself—that there was concern with, in one sense, *helping* the people selected. They were to be helped to overcome their false ideals, outmoded thoughts and outlooks, and Western influences on their thinking. However painful the treatment might be, essentially it was done *for* the person. This was, of course, one of the factors which made it doubly hard to resist.

The "old" person was to die and be reborn. This was emphasized both by the official doctrine and by the personal experiences of the participants. By various highly unpleasant means they first lost touch with their former identities and then found it possible to obtain the new ones which were held out before them. The theme of death and re-birth was a dominant one, emphasizing a total re-creation of the ego.

It is difficult to be neutral about some of the unpleasant and agonizing experiences described, yet this was no mere case of simple brutality or vengeance on a former oppressor class; it was—as Lifton notes—*totalist therapy*. It was therapy without constraints. It was done for the subject's own good (except for a few occasions with apparently personal motivation), but with *no limitations on what could be done to improve him.* As such it was superficially similar but basically entirely different from situations equally extreme, such as the concentration camps of World War II. For, as Lifton notes, the subject was never given the opportunity of viewing his own suffering as obviously noble and his oppressors as obviously base.

All of these points illustrate that the experiences were in fact intended as the treatment of an individual's problem. It was, to be sure, to the "benefit of the people" to have an important person re-educated, but it was also, in some strange way, seen to benefit that individual.[71] Although this aspect had important

71. See also Szasz, 1961, *op cit.*; on p. 208, he examines confessions of witchcraft as "therapeutic." All history teaches us that defining treatment as for the person's own good by no means insures that the person will appreciate the treatment offered. Even the Spanish Inquisition with its *auto-da-fe* (burning to death) could be justified as therapeutic. The Inquisition was for the good of the subject's immortal soul—better a brief pain now than the

effects in weakening resistance in the subject (and also, in all probability, in steeling the cadre to their tasks), it is important to us here in other ways. It demonstrates the social problem dimension as well as the existence of a therapeutic intention.[72] And in the selection of the person to be helped, the conception of the nature of the problem to be solved, and the types of personal changes sought, the phenomenon of systematic thought reform (or "brainwashing" or "ideological remolding") exemplifies the ideological basis of "treatment". It also demonstrates once again that one person's solution to a social problem is another person's brand new problem in itself.

A WESTERN DEBATE ON IDEOLOGY AND TREATMENT

An exploration of this phenomenon is incomplete without noticing a similar strain toward such total remaking of the personality in recent delinquency rehabilitation programmes in the West. In at least one case the analogy has been directly drawn between such programmes and the total therapy of brainwashing, and the ideological basis subjected to challenge. In 1962, a letter written to the *American Sociological Review* raised important questions respecting the Provo Experiment in delinquency rehabilitation.[73] It is couched in the rhetoric of the cold war era, but its message is still strikingly pertinent.

> *I suspect that many of us who have read the Empey and Rabow article on "The Provo Experiment in Delinquency Rehabilitation" have been profoundly impressed by it.... It is within such a framework that I should like to raise a not unsympathetic question.*

---

everlasting torments in Hell which the Inquisition foresaw for the eternally damned heretic. The subject was "questioned" until he confessed and recanted his sins, thus salvaging his soul before his execution.

72. Lifton, *op. cit.*, p. 15.

73. For a description of the programme, see Lamar T. Empey and Jerome Rabow, "The Provo Experiment in Delinquency Rehabilitation," *American Sociological Review*, 26, 1961, pp. 679-695.

In many ways—some of them superficial and some of them not—the techniques used at Pinehills [Provo] are reminiscent of those employed by the Communists in Korea on selected groups of American prisoners of war. One sees the leverage of the group being applied to the individual by way of public confessions, the demand for candor, the infinite patience and inscrutability of authority. There appears the "carrot and stick" technique along with the utilization of role disruption and social anxiety as motivating forces. Beyond that, one is reminded how systematically and thoroughly the integrity of psychological privacy is undermined.

I do not doubt that Empey and Rabow [the organizers of Provo] are fully aware of the parallels between their work and the efforts of the Communists in Korea.

The question which I should like to raise is the obvious one of values. In Korea we were shocked at what seemed to us the cynicism with which American was turned upon American. . . . We perceived something Orwellian and "ghoulish" in the "Rectification Program." I do not wish to suggest that intellectual consistency and ethical gentility require that we dismantle such programs as Empey and Rabow's. Far from it. . . . What I should urge is that we once again return to the classic question of means and ends. . . .

I raise the question and do not propose an answer—an old but honest academic trick. Before we are caught in the position of many nuclear physicists, I should like to urge that we think through with honesty quite what we are doing and what precedents we are establishing. It would be a supreme indictment of the students of society were we not to profit a priori from another social group now often tortured and troubled by its awesome contribution to the modern world.[74]

In their response to this letter, Empey and Rabow raised equally important considerations.[75] They first point out cor-

---

74. Whitney H. Gordon, "Communist Rectification Programs and Delinquency Rehabilitation Programs: A Parallel?" (Communication), *American Sociological Review*, 27, 1962, p. 256.
75. Lamar T. Empey and Jerome Rabow, "Reply to Whitney H. Gordon," *American Sociological Review*, 27, 1962, pp. 256-258.

rectly that many of the psycho-social dynamics which the Provo programme and "rectification" programmes share are also employed in other social practices, many of them quite traditional and legitimate. They mention the stress of students in universities, of recruits in the military. In other words, these processes appear all the time. Even the earlier gang-based socialization of delinquents (e.g., into toughness roles) is accomplished with considerable stress and strain. But Lifton has elsewhere pointed out that, although we can see certain limited aspects of brainwashing in advertising programmes, preparatory schools, or congressional investigations, and can therefore see a continuity between total therapy and less extreme programmes, this does not satisfactorily resolve the issue. As he puts it:

> [*Thought reform*] *has in fact emerged as one of the most powerful efforts at human manipulation ever undertaken. To be sure, such a program is by no means completely new: imposed dogmas, inquisitions, and mass conversion movements have existed in every country and during every historical epoch. But ... [thought reform has] a more organized, comprehensive, and deliberate—a more total—character, as well as a unique blend of energetic and ingenious psychological techniques.*[76]

It is perhaps the last point which is most relevant here: in contrast to earlier historical efforts, we now have some idea of what is happening when we manipulate in this way. With this knowledge, as the phrase goes, comes a heightening of power.

Empey and Rabow are probably on firmer grounds with their next point: what are the consequences of *not* changing these persons' lives? They point to the probability of years spent in confinement, the cruelty, the hostility, the sense of waste and futility—all of which would be part of the normal expectancies of the subjects of the Provo experiment in the absence of effective treatment. To be sure this also implies an ideological stance (i.e., that leading a non-delinquent life and staying out of

76. Lifton, *op. cit.*, pp. 4-5.

prison will make the individual happier), but they are correct in noting that failure to intervene, or to do so effectively, also has its consequences, and that in all likelihood many of these consequences would be considered undesirable from the subject's own standpoint.

Finally, the two authors emphasize what they see as critical differences between their approach and thought reform. Admitting that Provo used stress and other mechanisms to break a person's unquestioned ties with old perspectives, they point out that Provo then brought out in a realistic way the outcomes the delinquents could reasonably expect under different approaches to life, including a delinquent career, and the defects of each—including the defects of "going straight." They see this as the presentation of several realistic alternatives, a feature that the Communist Chinese programmes avoided.

Empey and Rabow might also have mentioned that the analogy may be a bit strained in terms of intensity, as Lifton's case studies graphically illustrate. We see no physiological symptoms of extreme anxiety, complete breakdowns, or suicides in the Provo experiment. The supreme sanction in Provo was transfer to the regular prison; the supreme sanction in Lifton's studies in China was death. The physical brutality which (only occasionally) entered the thought reform system had no analogue at Provo.[77]

The debate over Provo brings into sharp relief some of the basic dilemmas of treatment. All involuntary treatment for social problems is permeated by much ideological and perceptual consideration, in contrast to the rational ameliorative and therapeutic justifications provided by the persons in charge. But *failure* to intervene also poses its own problems. Assuming a consensus that a social problem exists, the three essential questions are: what constitutes adequate justification for involuntary treatment; what constitutes appropriate criteria for differential treatment; and what sorts of treatment are ethically permissible?

77. It is perhaps worth noting that neither "Provo" nor thought reform were as effective as was apparently hoped for, or feared.

SUMMARY

In previous chapters we looked at how both self-conscious, well articulated ideologies and vague but powerful stereotypes shape the definition of social problems. The present chapter expands this explanation into questions of how individuals are selected for "treatment" on the basis of stereotype and ideology. The term "treatment" is placed in quotation marks because there can be considerable differences of opinion as to what constitute reasonable ways to handle people. We have concentrated on the involuntary treatments that powerful viewpoints can impose on individuals.

In society's reaction to crime, discretion within the criminal justice system can be invoked at several points. Both judicial and police discretion are unavoidable if a desirable flexibility is to be achieved, but this same latitude for discretion leaves the door open for abuse. Tendencies of many judges and police to follow stereotypes and unspoken prejudices in their discretionary decisions is by now extremely well documented. Such miscarriages apparently hinge on both the individual's personal characteristics and political affiliations, with significant consequences. In police conduct and treatment it is clear that the demeanour of suspects (and of others at the scene) is also a major influence. The self-fulfilling nature of stereotypes, through differential enforcement practices, must also be considered.

Discussion next turned to selection and treatment for mental disorder. The extremely slipshod and careless manner in which vitally important commitment decisions are made has been documented again and again. Procedural safeguards that are accepted without question in courts of law are completely absent because of the legal fiction that involuntary commitment is non-punitive. The power dimension is often ignored in commitment, as is the possibility of covert motivations on the part of relatives or associates. Rosenhan's oft-cited research on the "stickiness" of mental labels once applied casts some doubt on the effectiveness of periodic formal reviews of those persons institutionalized.

Unconscious stereotyping makes an appearance in several disparities between social classes in psychiatric treatment.

Although major differences in diagnosis by social class may be partly a function of real differences brought on by the life experiences of each class, the same cannot be said of class differences in treatment within each diagnostic category, differences in the competence of personnel assigned, or differences in length of hospital stay. Stereotyping affects the situation from more than one direction: patients of different class backgrounds have distinct views about psychiatrists, and the upper middle class psychiatrists have vague but influential views about people from classes different from their own. All of these preconceptions influence the treatment provided.

Conscious ideology is also a factor in selection of persons for involuntary commitment. Several documented cases have surfaced in the West, while Soviet misuse of "sane asylums" to get rid of dissidents is well developed and advanced. Conscious ideology also has selected large numbers of people for reeducation or "thought reform" in China under the communist government. In all such cases, a divergence of views is present between those who regard the use of such measures as a solution to some social problem (troublesome, trouble-making people) and those who regard the measures themselves as social problems in their own right.

Moral dilemmas in treatment are highlighted when one notices uncomfortable convergences between "rehabilitation" programmes in the West (especially the more sophisticated projects) and inhumane, clearly abhorrent "rectification programmes." Are we merely reluctant to acknowledge these similarities because we accept the basis for treatment in the one case (delinquency) and not in the other (bourgeois background)? Is this complacency merely a result of our own outlook, which says that the state may re-mold delinquents but not re-mold adults who disagree with the party in power? Or is the analogy not so close because of real differences in treatment? This chapter as a whole should raise some serious ethical issues for the perceptive reader.

8 The Final Analysis

In the final analysis, there are some inescapable "facts of life" in the study of social problems. The very notion of a social problem has, as we have seen, a developmental history in Western thought. In certain periods social problems have been variously attributed to the individual's sinfulness, to malevolent spirits, or, in later periods, to an inferior heredity. The idea that iniquitous conditions are the responsibility of society as a whole, or that such conditions are not inherent, unchangeable aspects of life, was anything but obvious less than a hundred years ago. Even today the idea that all deleterious conditions are resolvable through some form of concerted social action is little more than an article of faith. (Indeed, as the labeling school of sociology would have it, the very attempts at amelioration are one of the sources of renewal for certain problems.)

The social problems notion emerged in a period with an almost unique combination of blatantly obvious suffering tied to the recognizable, novel conditions of urbanization and industrialization. But the cultural traditions of the period were equally essential: an unbounded optimistic faith in progress, and in the power of human reason, together leading to the idea of a social science that could rectify the social problems of the world as natural science was resolving physical problems. Not all social problems have emerged into public consciousness at the same time; the egalitarian drives for legal equality, abolition of slavery, social welfare legislation, women's rights, civil rights, and anti-colonialism are all more or less linked to specific periods in the last two hundred years. On the borders of consciousness today are new drives—for example, for the rights of children and the elderly.[1]

1. See for instance V.W. Marshall, *Aging in Canada*, Toronto: Fitzhenry &

Not only does the very modern idea of social problems itself have historical roots, but different specific social problems have each followed their own unique developmental patterns of thinking—as we saw by tracing the evolution of ideas about our two case studies, mental illness and poverty. The historical approach employed there could easily be turned on a host of other commonly accepted social problems, each illuminating a sometimes strange course of development of ideas. Nor need we feel smug, believing perhaps that the re-thinking process evident in the history of mental illness and poverty has ended; the sometimes startling new challenges to the conventional wisdom about present-day psychiatric treatment should warn us that the re-thinking will continue.

Just what is a social problem? We explored the difficulties encountered with this concept. Certainly one aspect exists when a significant number of individuals are adversely affected by a phenomenon, or believe that they are. And, for this to be a social problem, we added the qualification that such a phenomenon be related to social factors, with respect to its origin and treatment. But this at once leads to complications, since all major problems have their social dimension: equal protection for all members of society, lack of stigma for blameless victims, and, at the heart of the matter, mobilization of the society to deal with the problem. Thus even physical diseases can have social problem aspects. But the most serious question is Blumer's conception of a social problem as the result of a definitional activity rather than an objective state of affairs. If people are starving and, hypothetically, do not regard this as a problem, is it one nonetheless? If only victims regard a certain phenomenon as a social problem, is it? Or does it take recognition by the society at large? If only non-victims regard the phenomenon as a problem, should they be allowed to impose this definition on willing "victims"? We then encounter such illogical oddities as victimless crimes. With such questions we enter, unwillingly,

---

Whiteside, 1980; Richard Farson, *Birthrights: A Bill of Rights for Children*, New York: Macmillan, 1974; *Children's Liberation*, edited by David Gottlieb, Englewood Cliffs, N.J.: Prentice-Hall, 1973.

the sticky morass of cultural and ethical relativism, in which there are no easy answers.

The question of what constitutes a social problem comes most clearly into focus in the criminal law, for after rejecting simplistic notions of crime as sin or wickedness we find competing virtues for legalistic conceptions and social conceptions of crime. The old divisions of crimes *mala in se* versus *mala prohibita* prove useful too, for it is clear that most criminal law today is the latter; while we yet still tend to think of crime as the former. It is in *mala prohibita* that the century's law explosion has taken place, and we can consider whether victimless crime is the one or the other. Certainly it is the closeness of such victimless activities to *mala prohibita* that make laws against them so hard to enforce—and so lucrative to organized crime.

There is that strange feature of the law that actions which are prohibited become immoral to many people (even sinful) simply by virtue of being illegal: we can in fact "legislate morality," in a peculiar sense, because what we legislate *becomes* morality. On the other hand, this is true only if the vast mass of citizenry cooperate. When a critical number of people continues to disobey a law, especially in the context of a victimless activity, then the law itself comes into disrepute, organized crime may be greatly encouraged, ordinary citizens incur criminal records; ultimately, as with Prohibition, the law itself must be repealed to avert social disaster. A central debate today asks what the effect on society would be of *decriminalizing* victimless crimes and/or other crimes *mala prohibita*.

Returning to our basic question, a current view is that a social problem can only be defined in terms of what the members of society feel. This has been called the public awareness conception (or the subjective conception) of social problems. But obviously this assumes a degree of unity in conception which the people in a society only rarely possess. In a way, it makes more sense to think of "social problem making" as a process of conflict in which people's definitions clash. In many cases the act of defining pits some individuals or groups against others. This process can be seen most clearly in the creation of criminal law, in which some moral entrepreneurs attempt to invoke the severe machinery of the law against a group which regards its actions as justifiable. Eventually one conception succeeds and most members of the population feel compelled to at least pay lip service to the now-established consensus. If the winners are a defining group, a new social problem appears (such as male chauvinism); if the victors are what we might call "removers," a social problem is erased—not because the condition has changed but because most people no longer view it as a problem (the sale of intoxicating beverages, e.g.). On the other hand the victorious group may represent the status quo—neither introducing nor removing anything from the prevailing list of social problems.

Obviously, how one reacts to a given condition depends upon how one experiences it: whether one is victimized by it, stands to gain from it at others' expense, or gains personally with no one else involved. Reactions also depend upon how severely one is victimized: activities in which a few are hurt terribly attract greater public outrage than white-collar crimes in which millions may be hurt a little bit—even though the aggregate damage may be far greater for the latter. Whether anything is ever done about the condition depends not only on how an abstract majority may feel but more directly on the moods of powerful decision makers and on the gate-keepers of mass communication. Although the power of the media can easily be exaggerated, its capacity in "agenda setting" is of the greatest importance. Coverage in the mass media can be manipulated directly by gate-keepers and through concentration of ownership, less directly by skillful bureaucratic propaganda and institutional advertising. Indirectly, it is also influenced by the requirements of event velocity or rhythm and by topicality, which inadvertently magnify the importance of some events and relegate others (possibly of greater significance) to obscurity.

Not only may those directly affected by a condition act to redefine it, other recognizable sectors of society also commonly intervene in this process. Moral entrepreneurs, the people who seek new legislation and new definitions on moral grounds, are frequently a powerful factor. In earlier periods their basis was exclusively religion (variously interpreted), and even today religious entrepreneurs are a continuing source of some new legislation and definitions. Religion and the state at one time virtually combined to produce social problems perspectives, and law, for society. Growing secularization has dramatically increased the definitional role of other sectors, so that today psychiatrically-based definitions, and an ever-expanding circle of egalitarianism, aided by the social gospel sector of organized religion, provide the focal points for modern moral entrepreneurs.

Key figures in the definitional process—both as definers and removers of social problems—are intellectuals and professionals, the social problem experts. Their role is definitely expanding, some would say decisively. As we hope was made clear in Chapter 6, no group can safely be granted the exclusive definitional prerogative, no matter how great its expertise or general learning. As a group the intelligentsia possesses self-interests, distinctive life experiences, and self-imposed social isolation which may set it at odds with the desires of the rest of society, not to mention the trained incapacities which blind it to alternative perspectives. Its training may in many cases be used to provide a poor substitute for often deficient empathy with others. The ambitions of intellectuals, and desires for empire building, militate against free expression of views which contradict peer opinions. This is not to say that the insights and understandings of such individuals may not be far superior to those of the people in the street, merely that they cannot be *universally depended upon*.

Throughout this book we have tried in numerous sections to emphasize the impact of life experiences on outlook. Whether it is judges (and juries), legislators making laws for us all, victims with direct experience, or intellectuals far removed but with (hopefully) broader vision, people's experiences affect their ideas even when they are convinced of the sheer logical development and complete independence of those ideas. This sociology of knowledge component in the creation and acceptance of ideas and outlooks is one reason why consensus throughout a community is so hard to obtain. A single society today is so complex and so differentiated that commonly shared experiences—experiences undergone by all, or even a majority—are really very few in number. That is why, on the one hand, the few experiences universally shared by a society (the Great Depression, for example, or the Second World War) have such striking effects on thinking, and why, on the other hand, in most instances consensus today on social problems matters is virtually impossible to obtain.

The basic theoretical approaches to social problems have varied in their recognition of the definitional and ideological aspects of their subject matter. The early (classical) social pathology of the 1900's was sublimely confident of its ability to distinguish what was wrong with society. Differentiation between sick and healthy features never seemed a matter worthy of discussion. Interestingly, although the new pathologists of today tend to condemn society as a whole, rather than particular individuals, they too seem devoid of any qualms, any uncertainty as to what is unhealthy. So too the theorists of social disorganization, although endowed with a far broader historical and cultural perspective, never seemed overly troubled by such concerns. It was with the advent of the conflict and deviance perspectives that the first systematic inklings as to the role of definition and ideology in the social problem scene emerged. Merton's paradigm of deviance, and its close connection with his conception of functional* and dysfunctional components of a given society, seemed to imply this. The conflict theorists explicitly recognized the value-laden basis of social problems in terms of administration of justice, and the ability of the strong to impose their definitions on the rest of society. The most recent approach, the labeling school, has made the definitional nature of social problems one of their central conceptions. One way to develop keener sensitivity to this difficulty, and just possibly to help resolve it, is via cross-cultural and historical analyses of social problems, a task which is at last getting under way.

Once a social problem definition has been made, it is common to select certain individuals for involuntary treatment in an attempt to resolve or diminish the problem. Such treatment may be informal (as with police street intervention) or highly formalized and structured, as in treatment for mental illness or criminal activity. It may have rigid procedural safeguards to prevent abuse or it may have virtually no safeguards at all. Again, we have a definitional component (a label) and a conflict over its applicability, but now it is specific individuals rather than groups, organizations or larger collectivities who are the subject of some sort of adversary process, whether reasonable or grossly unfair. As we have seen, both the process of selection of particular individuals and the nature of their subsequent treatment are dependent not only on personal attributes or past behaviours which are legitimately connected with the problem but also on extraneous, irrelevant personal attributes, on political affiliations, or on the basis of group stereotypes. The hard evidence showing such intrusions into supposedly fair, objective decisions about a person's fate has become overwhelming. In addition to unconscious stereotypes, there are numerous occasions when well-formulated ideologies can also be seen at work in the selecting of particular individuals for treatment. And the mere fact that a treatment is undertaken for the subject's own good, however defined, is no guarantee of decency in a situation allowing totalist therapy.

These limitations—the questionable nature of social problems, the conflicting and changeable definitions that emerge, the ideological basis of treatment of individuals—do not mean that one should stand aside from the study of social problems. They do represent important considerations, learned at no small cost. In the final analysis, these perspectives on social problems can be disregarded only at the peril of the very humanitarian concerns which impel persons to do their work in the area.

Glossary

Acculturation In anthropology this term refers to the process of acquisition of culture that occurs when two or more societies come into contact. The term has been widely used to designate what took place in colonized societies where the indigenous cultures acquired many traits of the colonizing societies from immigrants, administrators, or missionaries. It can also imply cultural exchange, as when Europeans borrowed traits from subordinate cultures.

Anomie (Anomy) "The term has three different, though related, meanings. These are (a) personal disorganization of the sort that results in a disoriented or lawless individual, with little reference to the rigidity of the social structure or the character of its norms; (b) social situations in which the norms themselves are in conflict and the individual runs into trouble in his efforts to conform to contradictory requirements; and (c) a social situation that, in the limiting case, contains no norms and one that is, in consequence, the contrary of 'society' as 'anarchy' is the contrary of 'government'." Robert Bierstedt, in *A Dictionary of the Social Sciences*, edited by Julius Gould and William L. Kolb, New York: Free Press, 1964, p. 29.

Cultural Relativism "The principle that one cannot understand, interpret, or evaluate social and social psychological phenomena meaningfully unless the phenomena under study are seen with special reference to the role they play" in the particular society or culture in which they are found. Thus, this principle "holds that the customs of one culture canot objectively or validly be judged superior to those of another." George A. Theodorson and Achilles G. Theodorson, *A Modern Dictionary of Sociology*, New York: Crowell, 1969, p. 94. A thorough presentation of the concept is found in Melville J. Herskovitz, *Man and His Works*, New York: Alfred A. Knopf, 1951, pp. 61-79.

Dynamic Inter-Relationships Those relationships implying a continuing reciprocal influence.

Dysfunctional See functional.

Elite In this book the term refers to a relatively small group of individuals who influence others or exert power over others in a given field. We therefore differentiate a political elite, an intellectual elite (the "cream" of the intelligentsia), an academic elite (usually included in the former category), a religious elite, and so on. A country's elite would be those selected individuals from these fields who are most influential and recognized as eminent. (A separate meaning of elite as those most talented in some way is not employed in the book.) See *intelligentsia* and *knowledge producers*.

Equilibrium Maintenance of a given state (balance) in some condition. Equilibrium does not mean that change in the condition never takes place; rather, when it takes place in one area of society, other areas also change so as to reinstate the balance that had been temporarily disrupted. In dynamic equilibrium, the condition undergoes continuous change and equilibration involves handling departures from a steady or constant rate of change.

Functional-Dysfunctional A social phenomenon or cultural element is functional for some system if it contributes to the adjustment or adaptation of the system. "Those observed consequences which lessen the adaptation or adjustment of the system" are dysfunctional. Robert K. Merton, *Social Theory and Social Structure*, revised edition, New York: The Free Press, 1957, pp. 57ff.

Ideology An ideology is "a system of ideas and judgments, which are explicit and generally organized; which serve to describe, explain, interpret or justify the situation of a group or collectivity; and which, largely on the basis of values, suggest a precise orientation to the historical action of this group or collectivity." Guy Rocher (*A General Introduction to Sociology*, Toronto: Macmillan, 1972, p. 103) is herein quoting F. Dumont, "Notes sur l'analyse des idéologies," *Recherches Sociographiques*, 4, 1963, pp. 155-165. See also Karl Mannheim, *Ideology and Utopia*, translated by Louis Wirth and Edward Shils, New York: Harvest Book, 1936.

Intelligentsia-Intellectual Intelligentsia was originally a Russian term that has several possible levels of inclusiveness. In this book it refers to those individuals who produce or disseminate knowledge, such as university professors, writers, scientists, literary critics and social commentators. The term "intellectuals" is more frequently used in everyday language; we use the two terms interchangeably. However, we are not including in our definition all professionals, as the concept is at times understood in Eastern Europe. Nor do we include all teachers: not all professionals and teachers produce knowledge. Most only disseminate it without adding anything, or simply apply it as it has been handed down to them. For a discussion of these terms see Ronald Berman, *America in the Sixties; An Intellectual History*, New York: Free Press, 1968, pp. 10-16. See *knowledge producers* and *elite*.

Knowledge Producers Knowledge producers are those individuals who advance knowledge in any field and disseminate it—although the latter function can be fulfilled by other persons such as magazine and journal writers. The term as used here is practically synonymous with intelligentsia. See *intelligentsia* and *elite*.

Mass (society, media) In this book, it refers to those societies in which the groups and the individuals are (1) serviced by standardized goods that are disseminated by advertising, (2) are reached uniformly by a network of communications media and, (3) therefore, have the potential to be uniformly informed, serviced, and to carry on very similar styles of life. The words mass media and mass production are key concepts in this definition. There are conceptions of the mass as the mechanized, technological society, and the bureaucratized society—both of which are implicit in our own definition, although we repudiate any value judgment attached to these conceptions.

Mass media will refer to newspapers, magazines, film, radio and television. They are called mass media (rather than simply media of communication) because they reach a great number of persons in a highly uniform manner. We are not differentiating these media from specialized (scientific) journals in this book, but this distinction is frequently made.

Unfortunately there is very little standardization in the use of these terms. Meanings highly divergent from ours have sometimes been employed. For a discussion of the various uses of "mass" in "mass society" see Daniel Bell, *The End of Ideology*, revised edition, New York: Free Press, 1962, pp. 22-38.

Power Social power, in one classical definition, refers to the capacity of persons or groups to implement their wishes in spite of resistance. The sociologist most frequently quoted with respect to this term is Max Weber. See, for instance, H.H. Gerth and C. Wright Mills, *From Max Weber: Essays in Sociology*, New York: Oxford University Press, 1958. Another theoretical treatment of power and related concepts and theories can be found in Peter M. Blau, *Exchange and Power in Social Life*, New York: Wiley, 1964.

Proletariat This word has been widely disseminated in the literature of sociology following Marx's influence. It formally designates persons whose only control over the means of economic production is their own labour power (obtaining wages), as distinguished from the bourgeoisie who control either capital (obtaining profits or interest) or land (obtaining rent). In common usage, it refers to the poor working class, especially the manual workers. There is recognition of an industrial proletariat and of an agricultural proletariat. In North American the latter would refer to paid agricultural workers.

Reference Group Those groups whose standards of judgment and evaluation furnish guidelines for persons in their behaviour or in their choice of alternatives. The persons "refer" to this group (or their *perception* of how the group sees things) in evaluating their behaviour and their self-image; thus they are their "reference" group. It need not be a group to which the person belongs, but one he or she admires and aspires to (a particular professional group, for instance). There are more complex definitions which differentiate aspects of the phenomenon. See T. Shibutani, *Society and Personality*, Englewood Cliffs, N.J.: Prentice-Hall, 1961, pp. 257-260.

Role Role may be defined as "a pattern of behavior associated with a distinctive social position, e.g., that of father, teacher, employer or patient. The *ideal* role prescribes the rights and duties belonging to a social position." Role behaviour as actually enacted may not correspond precisely with the ideal role. Leonard Broom and Philip Selznick, *Sociology*, fourth edition, New York: Harper & Row, 1968, p. 18. See also *status*.

Self-Fulfilling Prophecy The self-fulfilling prophecy is "a false definition of the situation evoking a new behavior which makes the originally false conception come *true*." Robert K. Merton, *op. cit.*, p. 423, italics in the original. For an extended treatment see Richard L. Henshel, "Self-Altering Predictions," in *Handbook of Futures Research*, edited by J. Fowles, Westport, Conn.: Greenwood Press, 1978.

Socialization The process by which a person learns and internalizes the ways of living and thinking of his/her culture and sub-culture. Typically the term also refers to "internalization," in which the person comes to accept the ways he/she has been taught as natural and automatic. Socialization usually refers to children as opposed to adults. When discussing the latter, the compound "adult socialization" is usually employed. One of the best sourcebooks on socialization is the *Handbook of Socialization Theory and Research*, edited by David A. Goslin, Chicago: Rand McNally, 1969.

Social Control Agencies "Those organizations empowered by society to deprive people and organizations of their material wealth, their liberty or their lives." From Lawrence W. Sherman, "Three Models of Organizational Corruption in Agencies of Social Control," *Social Problems*, 27, 1980, pp. 478-488. Quoted is p. 479.

Social Movements Social movements can be defined as a wide variety of collective efforts to bring about an enduring change in society. See Guy Rocher, *op. cit.*, pp. 441-447. For an extended treatment see Armand L. Mauss, *Social Problems as Social Movements*, Philadelphia: Lippincott, 1975.

Status This concept has two meanings; although related, they are distinguished by the context in which the word is found. (1) "Status may refer simply to a person's social position. Each role in society is associated with a social position or status." For example, a prison guard has certain rights and responsibilities. These rights and duties together constitute his role (see definition of *role*); his position or status is that of prison guard. (2) "Status is also used to designate an individual's place within a system of social ranking." For instance, we may say that a person has high status in a group. Broom and Selznick, *op. cit.*, p. 44.

Stereotype-Stereotypy "Whether favorable or unfavorable, a stereotype is an exaggerated belief associated with a category [of individuals]." For instance, stereotypes can be exaggerated beliefs about Mexicans, Catholics, women, blacks, young persons, etc. "Its function is to justify (rationalize) our conduct in relation to that category." Gordon W. Allport, *The Nature of Prejudice*, Garden City: Doubleday, 1954, p. 187. Stereotypy refers to the processes of creating and using stereotypes.

Technology This term has two meanings, one mainly industrial, one predominantly anthropological. In the latter, technology encompasses the means people has at their disposition to exploit their environment (natural and manmade) in order to obtain food, shelter, clothing, and all the material objects of their culture. This implies, above all, tools and instruments, as well as the knowledge to design and operate them. In this interpretation, the term applies to all societies, for even in simple societies there is a technology. The terms "primitive" and "modern" technology are sometimes used. In this sense, all societies are technological.

The second meaning of technology, as in "technological society," is that of sophisticated and complex means to exploit the environment, applying principally to industrialized societies of the twentieth century. This meaning is prevalent in lay literature, as well as in social commentary. See *mass society*.

Value According to Kluckhohn, a value is "a conception, explicit or implicit, distinctive of an individual or characteristic of a group, of the desirable which influences the selection from available modes, means, and ends of action." Clyde Kluckhohn, "Values and Value-Orientations in the Theory of Action," in *Toward A General Theory of Action*, edited by Talcott Parsons and Edward A. Shils, New York: Harper Torchbooks, 1951, p. 395.

References

Adams, I., *The Poverty Wall*, Toronto: McClelland and Stewart, 1970.

Adams, I., *et al.*, *The Real Poverty Report*, Edmonton: Hurtig, 1971.

Allen, A.R., *The Social Passion: Religion and Social Reform in Canada, 1914-1928*, Toronto: University of Toronto Press, 1971.

Allport, G.W., *The Nature of Prejudice*, Garden City: Doubleday, 1954.

Altheide, D.L. and J.M. Johnson, *Bureaucratic Propaganda*, Boston: Allyn and Bacon, 1980.

Ambert, A.-M., "Differences in Children's Behavior Toward Custodial Mothers and Custodial Fathers," *Journal of Marriage and the Family*, 44, 1982, pp. 73-86.

Ambert, A.-M., *Divorce in Canada*, Toronto: Academic Press Canada, 1980.

Ambert, A.-M., *Sex Structure*, second edition revised and expanded, Toronto: Academic Press Canada, 1976.

Amnesty International report, *Prisoners of Conscience in the USSR: Their Treatment and Conditions*, second edition, London: Amnesty International Publications, 1980.

Anderson, C.H. and J.D. Murray, eds., *The Professors*, Cambridge: Schenkman, 1971.

Aronson, E.E., *The Social Animal*, third edition, San Francisco: Freeman, 1980.

Ausubel, D.P., "Personality Disorder is Disease," *American Psychologist*, 16, 1961, pp. 69-74.

Baldwin, B.A., *et al.*, "Status Inconsistency and Psychiatric Diagnoses: A Structural Approach to Labeling Theory," *Journal of Health and Social Behavior*, 16, 1975, pp. 257-267.

Baritz, L., *The Servants of Power*, New York: Wiley, 1965.

Baruch, G. and A. Treacher, *Psychiatry Observed*, Boston: Routledge, 1978.

Bazelon, D.T., *The Paper Economy*, New York: Vintage Books, 1965.

Becker, H.S., "The Marijuana Tax Act," in *Outsiders: Studies in the Sociology of Deviance*, by H.S. Becker, New York: Free Press, 1963.

Becker, H.S., *Outsiders: Studies in the Sociology of Deviance*, New York: Free Press, 1963.

Becker, H. and H.E. Barnes, *Social Thought from Lore to Science*, third edition, New York: Dover, 1961.

Bell, D., *The Coming of Post-Industrial Society*, New York: Basic Books, 1973.

Bell, D., "Crime as an American Way of Life," *Antioch Review*, 13, 1953, pp. 131-154.

Bell, D., *The End of Ideology*, revised edition, New York: Free Press, 1962.

Bell, W. and J.A. Mau, "Images of the Future: Theory and Research Strategies," in *The Sociology of the Future*, edited by W. Bell and J.A. Mau, New York: Russell Sage, 1971.

Bendix, R., "The Image of Man in the Social Sciences: The Basic Assumptions of Present-Day Research," *Commentary*, 11, 1951, pp. 187-192.

Bequai, A., *White-Collar Crime: A 20th Century Crisis*, Lexington, Mass.: Lexington Books, 1978.

Berelson, B. and G.F. Steiner, *Human Behavior: An Inventory of Scientific Findings*, New York: Harcourt, 1964.

Berger, P.L. and T. Luckmann, *The Social Construction of Reality*, Garden City, N.Y.: Doubleday, 1966.

Berkowitz, L., ed., *Roots of Aggression*, New York: Atherton, 1969.

Berman, R., *America in the Sixties; An Intellectual History*, New York: Free Press, 1968.

Bernard, J., *Social Problems at Midcentury*, New York: Dryden, 1957.

Bibby, R.W., "Consensus in Diversity: An Examination of Canadian Problem Perception," *International Journal of Comparative Sociology*, 20, 1979, pp. 274-282.

Bienvenue, R. and A.H. Latif, "Arrests, Dispositions and Recidivism: A Comparison of Indians and Whites," *Canadian Journal of Criminology and Corrections*, 16, 1974, pp. 105-116.

Bierstedt, R., "Anomie," in *A Dictionary of the Social Sciences*, edited by J. Gould and W.L. Kolb, New York: Free Press, 1964, p. 29.

Blackstock, N., *COINTELPRO: The FBI's Secret War on Political Freedom*, New York: Random House, 1975.

Blau, P.M., *Exchange and Power in Social Life*, New York: Wiley, 1964.

Blissett, M., *Politics in Science*, Boston: Little, Brown, 1972.

Blum, A.F., "Methods for Recognizing, Formulating, and Describing Social Problems," in *Handbook on the Study of Social Problems*, edited by E.O. Smigel, Chicago: Rand McNally, 1971.

Blumer, H., "Social Problems as Collective Behavior," *Social Problems*, 18, 1971.

Bohannan, P., ed., *Divorce and After*, New York: Doubleday, 1970.

Boorstin, D.J., *Image: A Guide to Pseudo-Events in America*, New York: Atheneum, 1962.

Bossard, J.H.S., *Social Change and Social Problems*, revised edition, New York: Harper and Brothers, 1938.

Boudreau, F., "The Quebec Psychiatric System in Transition: A Case Study in Psychopolitics," *Canadian Review of Sociology and Anthropology*, 17, 1980, pp. 122-137.

Bouma, G.D. and W.J. Bouma, *Fertility Control: Canada's Lively Social Problem*, Toronto: Academic Press Canada, 1975.

Bowen, D., *The Protestant Crusade in Ireland, 1800-1870*, Montreal: McGill-Queens University Press, 1978.

Boydell, C.L. and C.F. Grindstaff, "Public Attitudes Toward Legal Sanctions for Drug and Abortion Offenses," *Canadian Journal of Criminology and Corrections*, 13, 1971, pp. 209-232.

Bradburn, N., *The Structure of Psychological Well-being*, Chicago: Aldine, 1969.

Brinton, C., "Humanitarianism," in *Encyclopedia of the Social Sciences*, New York: Macmillan, 1932, vol. 7, pp. 544-548.

Broom, L. and P. Selznick, *Sociology*, fourth edition, New York: Harper & Row, 1968.

Bruce-Briggs, B., ed., *The New Class?*, New Brunswick, N.J.: Transaction Books, 1979.

Bruner, J.S., "On Perceptual Readiness," in *Current Perspectives in Social Psychology*, edited by E.P. Hollander and R.G. Hunt, New York: Oxford University Press, 1963, pp. 42-47.

Bullock, H.A., "Significance of the Racial Factor in the Length of Prison Sentence," *Journal of Criminal Law, Criminology and*

Police Science, 52, 1961, pp. 411-417.

Burch, W.R., Jr., "Images of Future Leisure: Continuities in Changing Expectations," in The Sociology of the Future, edited by W. Bell and J.A. Mau, New York: Russell Sage, 1971.

Canadian Council on Children and Youth, Admittance Restricted: The Child as Citizen in Canada, Ottawa: 1978.

Cannabis (LeDain Report), Report of the Commission of Inquiry into the Non-Medical Use of Drugs, Ottawa: Information Canada, 1972.

Caplan, R.B., Psychiatry and the Community in Nineteenth-Century America, New York: Basic Books, 1969.

Cardinal, H., The Unjust Society: The Tragedy of Canada's Indians, Edmonton: M.G. Hurtig, 1969.

Carrier, Le Sociologue Canadien Léon Gérin, 1863-1951, Montreal: Bellarmin, 1959.

Caskie, D., The Canadian Fact Book on Poverty, Ottawa: Canadian Council on Social Development, 1979.

Chesler, P., "Patient and Patriarch: Women in the Psychotherapeutic Relationship," in Women in Sexist Society, edited by V. Gornick and B.K. Moran, New York: Basic Books, 1971.

Chiricos, T.G., et al., "Inequality in the Imposition of a Criminal Label," Social Problems, 19, 1972, pp. 553-572.

Cicourel, A.V., The Social Organization of Juvenile Justice, New York: Wiley, 1968.

Clark, J.P., "Isolation of the Police: A Comparison of British and American Situations," Journal of Criminal Law, Criminology, and Police Science, 56, 1965, pp. 307-319.

Clinard, M.B., Anomie and Deviant Behavior: A Discussion and Critique, New York: Free Press, 1964.

Cloward, R.A. and L.E. Ohlin, Delinquency and Opportunity, New York: Free Press, 1966.

Cocozza, J.J. and H.J. Steadman, "Prediction in Psychiatry: An Example of Misplaced Confidence in Experts," Social Problems, 23, 1978, pp. 265-276.

Cohen, A.K., Delinquent Boys, New York: Free Press, 1955.

Coll, B.D., Perspectives in Public Welfare: A History, Washington: United States Department of Health, Education and Welfare, 1969.

Connor, D.M. and J.E. Curtis, Sociology and Anthropology in Canada, Montreal: Canadian Sociology and Anthropology

Association, September, 1970.

Conrad, P. and J. Schneider, *Deviance and Medicalization: From Badness to Sickness*, St. Louis, Mo.: Mosby, 1980.

Cook, S.J., "Canadian Narcotics Legislation, 1908-1923: A Conflict Model Interpretation," *Canadian Review of Sociology and Anthropology*, 6, 1969, pp. 36-46.

Cooper, D., *The Death of the Family*, New York: Vintage Books, 1970.

Coser, L.A., *The Functions of Social Conflict*, New York: Free Press, 1966.

Coser, L.A., "Sociology of Poverty," *Social Problems*, 13, 1965, pp. 140-148.

Cousineau, D.F. and J. Veevers, "Incarceration as a Response to Crime: The Utilization of Canadian Prisons," *Canadian Journal of Criminology and Corrections*, 14, 1972, pp. 10-36.

Crane, D., "The Gatekeepers of Science: Some Factors Affecting the Selection of Articles for Scientific Journals," *American Sociologist*, 2, 1967, pp. 195-201.

Crane, D., "Scientists at Major and Minor Universities: A Study of Productivity and Recognition," *American Sociological Review*, 32, 1965, pp. 377-390.

Creal, M., *The Idea of Progress*, Agincourt, Ont.: Macmillan, 1970.

Cross, M., *The Workingman in the Nineteenth Century*, Toronto: Oxford University Press (Readings in Canadian Social History Series), 1974.

Dahrendorf, R., *Class and Class Conflict in Industrial Society*, Stanford University Press, 1959.

Dain, N., *Concepts of Insanity in the United States 1759-1865*, New Brunswick, N.J.: Rutgers University Press, 1964.

Daniels, A.K., "Professional Responses to 'Insider' Critics: Psychiatrists Consider Dr. Szasz," paper presented at the annual meeting of the Society for the Study of Social Problems, New Orleans, 1972.

Davis, F.J., "Crime News in Colorado Newspapers," *American Journal of Sociology*, 57, 1952, pp. 325-330.

Davis, F.J. and R. Stivers, eds., *The Collective Definition of Deviance*, New York: Free Press, 1975.

Dentler, R.A., *Major Social Problems*, second edition, Chicago: Rand McNally, 1972.

Djao, A.W., "The Welfare State and Its Ideology," in *Economy, Class and Social Reality*, edited by J.A. Fry, Toronto: Butterworths, 1979.

Drapkin, I. and E. Viano, eds., *Victimology: A New Focus*, vols. I and II, Lexington, Mass.: Lexington Books, 1973.

Drucker, P.F., *The Age of Discontinuity*, New York: Harper and Row, 1969.

Dumont, F., "Notes sur l'analyse des idéologies," *Recherches Sociographiques*, 4, 1963, pp. 155-165.

Durkheim, E., *Suicide*, Glencoe, Ill.: Free Press, 1951 (1897).

Dussuyer, I., *Crime News: A Study of 40 Ontario Newspapers*, Toronto: University of Toronto Centre of Criminology, 1979.

Eisenstadt, S.N., ed., *Comparative Social Problems*, New York: Free Press, 1964.

Empey, L.T. and J. Rabow, "The Provo Experiment in Delinquency Rehabilitation," *American Sociological Review*, 26, 1961, pp. 679-695.

Empey, L.T. and J. Rabow, "Reply to Whitney H. Gordon," *American Sociological Review*, 27, 1962, pp. 256-258.

Erikson, E., "The Nature of Clinical Evidence," in *Evidence and Inference*, edited by Daniel Lerner, Glencoe, Ill.: Free Press, 1959, pp. 73-95.

Erikson, K.T., *Wayward Puritans*, New York: Wiley, 1966.

Etzioni, A., "Toward a Theory of Societal Guidance," *American Journal of Sociology*, 73, 1967, pp. 173-187.

Etzioni, A. and R. Remp, *Technological Shortcuts in the Treatment of Social Problems*, New York: Russell Sage, 1972.

Eysenck, H., *The Effects of Psychotherapy*, New York: International Science Press, 1966.

Falardeau, J.-C., *Etienne Parent, 1802-1874*, Montreal: La Presse, 1974.

Falardeau, J.-C., *L'essor des sciences sociales au Canada français*, Québec: Ministère des affaires culturelles, 1964.

Farrington, D.P., "The Effects of Public Labelling," *British Journal of Criminology*, 17, 1977, pp. 112-126.

Farson, R., *Birthrights: A Bill of Rights for Children*, New York: Macmillan, 1974.

Fein, S. and K.S. Miller, "Legal Process and Adjudication in Mental Incompetency Proceedings," *Social Problems*, 20, 1972, pp. 57-64.

Feldman, S.D., *Deciphering Deviance*, Boston: Little, Brown, 1978.

Festinger, L., *et al.*, *When Prophecy Fails*, Minneapolis: University of Minnesota Press, 1956.

A. Finkel, "Origins of the Welfare State in Canada," in *The Canadian State*, edited by L. Panitch, Toronto: University of Toronto Press, 1977.

Fishman, G., "Can Labelling be Useful?" in *Youth Crime and Juvenile Justice*, edited by P.C. Friday and V.L. Stewart, New York: Praeger, 1977.

Fishman, M., "Crime Waves as Ideology," *Social Problems*, 25, 1978, pp. 531-543.

Fishman, M., *Manufacturing the News*, Austin: University of Texas Press, 1980.

Fortin, G., "Le Québec: Une société globale à la recherche d'elle-même," *Recherches Sociographiques*, 8, 1967, pp. 7-13.

Foucault, M., *Madness and Civilization. A History of Insanity In The Age of Reason*, translated by Richard Howard, New York: Random House, 1965.

Fournier, M. and G. Houle, "La sociologie québécoise et son objet: problématiques et débats/Quebec Sociology and its Object: Problematics and Debates," *Sociologie et Sociétés*, 12, 1980, pp. 21-44.

Frank, P.K., *The Anti-psychiatry Bibliography/Resource Guide*, Vancouver: Press Gang Publishers, 1979.

Friedman, L.M., *Government and Slum Housing: A Century of Frustration*, Chicago: Rand McNally, 1968.

Friedrichs, R., *A Sociology of Sociology*, New York: Free Press, 1970.

Fuller, R.C., "Sociological Theory and Social Problems," *Social Forces*, 15, 1937, pp. 496-502.

Galbraith, J.K., "An Adult's Guide to New York, Washington and Other Exotic Places," *New York*, November 15, 1971, p. 52.

Galbraith, J.K., *The New Industrial State*, Boston: Houghton Mifflin, 1967.

Galtung, J. and M. Ruge, "Structuring and Selecting News," in *The Manufacture of News*, edited by S. Cohen and J. Young, Beverly Hills: Sage, 1973.

Gandy, J.M., "The Exercise of Discretion by the Police as a

Decision-Making Process in the Disposition of Juvenile Offenders," *Osgoode Hall Law Journal*, 8, 1970, pp. 333-346.

Gans. H., *Deciding What's News*, New York: Pantheon Books, 1979.

Gans, H., "The Positive Functions of Poverty," *American Journal of Sociology*, 78, 1972, pp. 275-289.

Garique, P., "French Canada: A Case Study in Sociological Analysis," *Canadian Review of Sociology and Anthropology*, 1, 1964, pp. 186-193.

Geis, G., *Not the Law's Business*, New York: Schocken Books, 1979.

George, P.M. and H.Y. Kim, "Social Factors and Educational Aspirations of Canadian High School Students," in *Social Process and Institution: The Canadian Case*, by J.E. Gallagher and R.D. Lambert, Toronto: Holt, Rinehart and Winston, 1971, pp. 352-363.

George, V. and P. Wilding, *Motherless Families*, London: Routledge, 1972.

Gerth, H.H. and C.W. Mills, *From Max Weber: Essays in Sociology*, New York: Oxford University Press, 1958.

Gibbs, J.P., "Conceptions of Deviant Behavior: The Old and the New," *Pacific Sociological Review*, 9, 1966, pp. 9-14.

Giddens, A., *The Class Structure of the Advanced Societies*, London: Hutchinson, 1973.

Giffen, P.J., "The Revolving Door: A Functional Interpretation," *Canadian Review of Sociology and Anthropology*, 3, 1966, pp. 154-166.

Goffman, E., *The Presentation of Self in Everyday Life*, Garden City, New York: Doubleday Anchor, 1959.

Goldstein, M.S., "The Sociology of Mental Health and Illness," in *Annual Review of Sociology*, vol. 5, edited by A. Inkeles *et al.*, La Jolla, Cal.: Annual Reviews, 1979.

Good, Bad, or Simply Inevitable? Selected Research Studies, vol. 3 of Report of the Special Committee on Mass Media, Ottawa: Information Canada, 1970.

Goode, M.R., "Law Reform Commission of Canada—political Ideology of Criminal Process Reform," *Canadian Bar Review*, 1976, pp. 653-674.

Gordon, W.H., "Communist Rectification Programs and Delinquency Rehabilitation Programs: A Parallel?" (Communication), *American Sociological Review*, 27, 1962, p. 256.

Goslin, D.A., ed., *Handbook of Socialization Theory and Research*, Chicago: Rand McNally, 1969.

Gottlieb, D., ed., *Children's Liberation*, Englewood Cliffs, N.J.: Prentice-Hall, 1973.

Gouldner, A.W., "Anti-Minotaur: the Myth of a Value-Free Sociology," *Social Problems*, 9, 1962, pp. 199-213.

Gouldner, A.W., *The Coming Crisis of Western Sociology*, New York: Basic Books, 1970.

Gouldner, A.W., "The Sociologist as Partisan: Sociology and the Welfare State," reprinted in *The Sociology of Sociology*, edited by L.T. Reynolds and J.M. Reynolds, New York: McKay, 1970.

Gove, W.R., ed., *The Labelling of Deviance*, New York: Sage, 1975.

Gove, W.R., "Societal Reaction as an Explanation of Mental Illness: An Evaluation," *American Sociological Review*, 35, 1970, pp. 873-884.

Green, E., *Judicial Attitudes in Sentencing*, London: Macmillan, 1961.

Greenglass, E., *After Abortion*, Toronto: Academic Press Canada, 1977.

Griffiths, C.T., *et al.*, *Criminal Justice in Canada: An Introductory Text*, Vancouver: Butterworth Western Canada, 1980.

Grosman, B., "The Discretionary Enforcement of Law," *Chitty's Law Journal*, 21, 1973.

Grosman, B., *Police Command: Decisions and Discretion*, Agincourt, Ontario: Macmillan of Canada, 1975.

Gross, M.L., *The Brain Watchers*, New York: Random House, 1962.

Gwynne-Timothy, J., *Quest for Democracy*, Vols. 1 and 2, Toronto: McClelland and Stewart, 1970.

Hackler, J.C., *The Prevention of Youthful Crime: The Great Stumble Forward*, Toronto: Methuen, 1978.

Hagan, J., *The Disreputable Pleasures*, Toronto: McGraw-Hill Ryerson, 1977.

Hagan, J.J., "The Labelling Perspective, the Delinquent, and the Police: A Review of the Literature," *Canadian Journal of Corrections*, 14, 1972, pp. 150-165.

Hakeem, M., "A Critique of the Psychiatric Approach to Crime and Corrections," Law and Contemporary Problems, 23, 1958, pp. 650-682.

Halmos, P., The Faith of the Counsellors, Don Mills, Ontario: Longman, 1965.

Hanly, C., Mental Health in Ontario, A Study for the Committee on the Healing Arts, Toronto: Queen's Printer, 1970.

Harp, J. and J.E. Curtis, "Linguistic Communication and Sociology: Data from the Canadian Case," in Social Process and Institution: The Canadian Case, by J.E. Gallagher and R.D. Lambert, Toronto: Holt, Rinehart and Winston of Canada, 1971, pp. 57-71.

Harp, J. and J.R. Hofley, eds., Poverty in Canada, Scarborough, Ont.: Prentice-Hall, 1971.

Harvey, F., "Préliminaires à une sociologie historique des maladies mentales au Québec," Recherches Sociographiques, 16, 1975, pp. 113-117.

Haskell, T.L., The Emergence of Professional Social Science, Urbana, Ill.: University of Illinois Press, 1977.

Hawkins, R. and G. Tiedeman, The Creation of Deviance, Columbus, Ohio: Charles Merrill, 1975.

Heberle, R., "Social Movements," in International Encyclopedia of the Social Sciences, New York: Crowell, Collier and Macmillan, 1986, vol. 14, p. 440.

Henry, F., Forgotten Canadians: The Blacks of Nova Scotia, Toronto: Academic Press Canada, 1973.

Henshel, R.L., "Effects of Disciplinary Prestige on Predictive Accuracy: Distortions from Feedback," Futures, Journal of Forecasting and Planning, 7, 1975, pp. 92-106.

Henshel, R.L., Reacting to Social Problems, Toronto: Academic Press Canada, 1976.

Henshel, R.L., "Self-Altering Predictions," in Handbook of Futures Research, edited by J. Fowles, Westport, Conn.: Greenwood Press, 1978.

Henshel, R.L. and R. Silverman, eds., Perception in Criminology, New York: Columbia University Press, 1975.

Herskovitz, M.J., Man and His Works, New York: Alfred A. Knopf, 1951.

Heussenstamm, F.K., "Bumper Stickers and the Cops," in Contemporary Social Psychology: Representative Readings, edited by T. Blass, Itasca, Ill.: Peacock, 1976, pp. 137-140.

Hilberg, R., "The Destruction of the European Jews," in *Mass Society in Crisis*, edited by B. Rosenberg *et al.*, New York: Macmillan, 1964.

Hinkle, R.C. and G. Hinkle, *The Development of Modern Sociology*, New York: Random House, 1962.

Hodge, R.W., *et al.*, "Occupational Prestige in the United States: 1925-1963," in *Class, Status, and Power*, second edition, edited by R. Bendix and S.M. Lipset, New York: Free Press, 1966.

Hoffer, E., *The True Believer; Thoughts on the Nature of Mass Movements*, New York: Harper & Row, 1951.

Hogarth, J., *Sentencing as a Human Process*, Toronto: University of Toronto Press, 1971.

Hollingshead, A.B. and F.C. Redlich, *Social Class and Mental Illness*, New York: Wiley, 1958.

Holzner, B. and J.H. Marx, *Knowledge Application: The Knowledge System in Society*, Boston: Allyn and Bacon, 1979.

Hopkins, C.H., *The Rise of the Social Gospel in American Protestantism, 1865-1915*, New Haven: Yale University Press, 1967.

Horowitz, I.L., *Professing Sociology*, Chicago: Aldine, 1968.

Horton, J., "Order and Conflict Theories of Social Problems," *American Journal of Sociology*, 71, 1966, pp. 701-713.

Horton, P.B. and G.R. Leslie, *The Sociology of Social Problems*, fourth edition, New York: Appleton-Century-Crofts, 1970.

Hoult, T.F., ". . . Who Shall Prepare Himself to the Battle?" *American Sociologist*, 3, 1968, pp. 3-7.

Inkeles, A., "Industrial Man: The Relation of Status to Experience, Perception, and Value," *American Journal of Sociology*, 66, 1961, pp. 1-31.

Jensen, G.F., "Labeling and Identity: Toward a Reconciliation of Divergent Findings," *Criminology*, 18, 1980, pp. 121-129.

Johanson, D. and M. Edey, *Lucy: The Beginnings of Humankind*, New York: Simon and Schuster, 1981.

Johnson, E.H., *Crime, Correction and Society*, revised edition, Homewood, Ill.: Dorsey Press, 1968.

Johnson, W.T., *et al.*, "Arrest Probabilities for Marijuana Users as Indicators of Selective Law Enforcement," *American Journal of Sociology*, 83, 1977, pp. 681-700.

Johnston, R. and D. Robbins, "The Development of Specialties in

Industrialized Science," *The Sociological Review*, 25 (New Series), 1977.

Jones, J.A., "Federal Efforts to Solve Contemporary Social Problems," in *Handbook on the Study of Social Problems*, edited by E.O. Smigel, Chicago: Rand McNally, 1971.

Joravsky, D., "Lysenkoism," *Scientific American*, 207, November, 1962, pp. 41-49.

Kadish, S.H., "The Crisis of Over-criminalization," *The Annals*, 374, 1967, pp. 157-170.

Kallen, E., *Spanning the Generations*, Toronto: Academic Press Canada, 1977.

Kavolis, V., *Comparative Perspectives on Social Problems*, Boston: Little, Brown, 1969.

Kelly, Monsignor G.A., *Overpopulation: A Catholic View*, New York: Paulist Press, 1960.

Kent, C., *Brains and Numbers: Elitism, Comtism, and Democracy in Mid-Victorian England*, Toronto: University of Toronto Press, 1978.

Kessler, R.C. and P.D. Cleary, "Social Class and Psychological Distress," *American Sociological Review*, 45, 1980, pp. 463-478.

Killian, L.M., "Optimism and Pessimism in Sociological Analysis," *American Sociologist*, 6, 1971, pp. 281-286.

Kittrie, N., *The Right to be Different*, Baltimore: Johns Hopkins University Press, 1971.

Klapp, O.E., *Currents of Unrest*, New York: Holt, Rinehart and Winston, 1972.

Klapper, J.T., *The Effects of Mass Communication*, Glencoe, Ill.: Free Press, 1959.

Kleinberg, B., *American Society in the Postindustrial Age*, Columbus, Ohio: Merrill, 1973.

Kluckhohn, C., "Values and Value-Orientations in the Theory of Action," in *Toward a General Theory of Action*, edited by T. Parsons and E.A. Shils, New York: Harper Torchbooks, 1951.

Koenig, D.J., "Police Perceptions of Public Respect and Extra-Legal Use of Force," *Canadian Journal of Sociology*, 1, 1975, pp. 313-324.

Krisberg, B., "The Sociological Imagination Revisited," *Canadian Journal of Criminology and Corrections*, 16, 1974, pp. 146-161.

Kutner, L., "The Illusion of Due Process in Commitment Proceedings," *Northwestern Law Review*, 57, 1962, pp. 383-399.

LaFave, W.R., *Arrest: The Decision to Take a Suspect into Custody*, Boston: Little, Brown, 1964.

Laing, R.D., *The Politics of Experience*, London: Penguin Books, 1967.

LaMarsh, J., *Report of Royal Commission on Violence in the Media*, Toronto: Queen's Printer, 1977.

Langner, T.S. and S.T. Michael, *Life Stress and Mental Health*, Glencoe, Ill.: Free Press, 1963.

Larrabee, E., "Scientists in Collision: Was Velikovsky Right?" *Harper's*, 227, August, 1963, pp. 48-55.

Lauer, R.H., "Defining Social Problems: Public and Professional Perspectives," *Social Problems*, 22, October, 1976, pp. 122-134.

Lazarsfeld, P.F. and W. Thielens, Jr., *The Academic Mind*, Glencoe, Ill.: Free Press, 1958.

Lemert, E.M., *Human Deviance, Social Problems, and Social Control*, Englewood Cliffs, N.J.: Prentice-Hall, 1967.

Lemert, E.M., *Social Pathology*, New York: McGraw-Hill, 1951.

Lemert, E., "Social Problems," *International Encyclopedia of the Social Sciences*, New York: Crowell, Collier and Macmillan, 1968, vol. 14, p. 455.

Liazos, A., "The Poverty of the Sociology of Deviance: Nuts, Sluts, and Preverts," *Social Problems*, 20, 1972, pp. 103-120.

Liem, R. and J. Liem, "Social Class and Mental Illness Reconsidered: The Role of Economic Stress and Social Support," *Journal of Health and Social Behavior*, 1978, 19, pp. 139-156.

Lifton, R.J., *Thought Reform and the Psychology of Totalism*, New York: Norton, 1969.

Lilienfeld, R., *The Rise of Systems Theory: An Ideological Perspective*, New York: Wiley, 1978.

Lin, N., "Stratification of the Formal Communication System in Science," paper presented at the annual meeting of the American Sociological Association, Denver, Colorado, August, 1971.

Lippmann, W., "The University," *The New Republic*, May 28, 1966, pp. 17-20.

Lipset, S.M. and R.B. Dobson, "The Intellectual as Critic and Rebel: With Special Reference to the United States and the

Soviet Union," *Daedalus*, 101, 1972, pp. 137-198.

Longfellow, C., "Divorce in Context: Its Impact on Children," in *Divorce and Separation*, edited by G. Levinger and O.C. Moles, New York: Basic Books, 1979.

Lowi, T.J., *The End of Liberalism—Ideology, Policy, and the Crisis of Public Authority*, New York: Norton, 1969.

Lundman, R.J., *et al.*, "Police Control of Juveniles: A Replication," *Journal of Research in Crime and Delinquency*, 15, January, 1978.

Lundman, R.J. and J.C. Fox, "Maintaining Research Access in Police Organizations," *Criminology*, 16, 1978, pp. 87-97.

MacDonald, D., "Communication: The State of the Canadian News Media," pp. 131-140 in G. Joch *et al.*, *Studies in Canadian Communications*, Montreal: McGill University Printing Service, 1975.

Mack, R.W., "Theoretical and Substantive Biases in Sociological Research," in *Interdisciplinary Relationships in the Social Sciences*, edited by M. and C. Sherif, Chicago: Aldine, 1969.

Mannheim, K., *Ideology and Utopia*, translated by L. Wirth and E. Shils, New York: Harvest Books, 1936.

Manning, P.K., "On Deviance," *Contemporary Sociology*, 2, 1973, pp. 123-128.

Manuel, F., *The Prophets of Paris*, Cambridge, Mass.: Harvard University Press, 1962.

Marshall, V.W., *Aging in Canada*, Toronto: Fitzhenry & Whiteside, 1980.

Mathews, R. and J. Steele, *The Struggle for Canadian Universities*, Toronto: New Press, 1970.

Mauss, A.L., *Social Problems as Social Movements*, Philadelphia: Lippincott, 1975.

McCall, G.J., *Observing the Law: Field Methods in the Study of Crime and the Criminal Justice System*, New York: Collier Macmillan, 1978.

McCormick, A.E., Jr., "Rule Enforcement and Moral Indignation," *Social Problems*, 25, 1977, pp. 30-39.

McDonald, L., *The Sociology of Law and Order*, Montreal: Book Centre, 1976.

McKee, J.B., "Some Observations on the Self-Consciousness of Sociologists," in *The Sociology of Sociology*, edited by L.T. Reynolds and J.M. Reynolds, New York: McKay, 1970.

McKerracher, D.G., *Trends in Psychiatric Care*, Royal Commission on Health Services, Ottawa: Queen's Printer, 1966.

McLuhan, M., "The Electronic Age—The Age of Implosion," in *Mass Media in Canada*, edited by J.A. Irvin, Toronto: Ryerson Press, 1962, pp. 179-205.

McNeely, R.L. and C.E. Pope, eds., *Race, Crime, and Criminal Justice*, Beverly Hills, Cal.: Sage, 1981.

Merton, R.K., "Priorities in Scientific Discovery: A Chapter in the Sociology of Science," *American Sociological Review*, 22, 1959, pp. 635-659.

Merton, R.K., "Social Problems and Sociological Theory," in *Contemporary Social Problems*, third edition, edited by R.K. Merton and R. Nisbet, New York: Harcourt Brace Jovanovich, 1971.

Merton, R.K., "Social Structure and Anomie," *American Sociological Review*, 3, 1939, pp. 672-682.

Merton, R.K., *Social Theory and Social Structure*, revised and enlarged edition, Glencoe, Ill.: Free Press, 1957.

Messner, H., ed., *Poverty In The Affluent Society*, New York: Harper and Row, 1966.

Miliband, R., *The State in Capitalist Society*, New York: Quartet Books, 1975.

Mills, C.W., "The Professional Ideology of Social Pathologists," in *Power, Politics and People*, by C.W. Mills, edited by I.L. Horowitz, New York: Ballantine Books, 1963 (original: 1943).

Milosz, C., *The Captive Mind*, translated by J. Zielonko, New York: Vintage Books, 1957.

Moore, B., Jr., *Reflections on the Causes of Human Misery*, Boston: Beacon, 1970.

Morgan, J.G., "Contextual Factors in the Rise of Academic Sociology in the United States," *Canadian Review of Sociology and Anthropology*, 7, 1970, pp. 159-171.

Morris, R. and C.M. Lanphier, *Three Scales of Inequality: Perspectives on French-English Relations*, Toronto: Academic Press Canada, 1977.

Myers, J.K. and L. Schaffer, "Social Stratification and Psychiatric Practice," *American Sociological Review*, 19, 1954, pp. 307-310.

Nagler, M., *Natives Without a Home: The Canadian Indian*, Toronto: Academic Press Canada, 1975.

Nettler, G., "Good Men, Bad Men, and the Perception of Reality," *Sociometry*, 24, 1961, pp. 279-294.

Newman, G., *Comparative Deviance: Perception and Law in Six Cultures*, New York: Elsevier, 1976.

Nietzsche, F., *Beyond Good and Evil*, Chicago: Henry Regnery, 1955 (1885).

Nisbet, R., *History of the Idea of Progress*, New York: Basic Books, 1980.

Ogburn, W.F., *Social Change*, New York: Heubsch, 1922.

Packer, H.L., *The Limits of the Criminal Sanction*, Stanford, Calif.: Stanford University Press, 1968.

Pasamanick, B., "The Development of Physicians for Public Mental Health," *American Journal of Orthopsychiatry*, 37, 1967, pp. 469-486.

Pedersen, E. and K. Etheridge, "Conformist and Deviant Behaviour in High School: The Merton Typology Adapted to an Educational Context," *Canadian Review of Sociology and Anthropology*, 7, 1970, pp. 70-82.

Petrunik, M., "The Rise and Fall of 'Labelling Theory': The Construction and Destruction of a Sociological Strawman," *Canadian Journal of Sociology*, 5, 1980, pp. 213-235.

Piliavin, I. and S. Briar, "Police Encounters with Juveniles," *American Journal of Sociology*, 70, 1964, pp. 206-214.

Piven, F.F. and R.A. Cloward, *Regulating the Poor: The Functions of Public Welfare*, New York: Random House, 1971.

Podhoretz, N., *Making It*, New York: Random House, 1967.

Poynter, J.R., *Society and Pauperism: English Ideas on Poor Relief, 1795-1834*, Toronto: University of Toronto Press, 1969.

Pratt, S. and J. Tooley, "Innovations in Mental Hospital Concepts and Practice," in *Major American Social Problems*, by R.A. Dentler, Chicago: Rand McNally, 1967.

President's Commission on Law Enforcement and Administration of Justice, *The Challenge of Crime in a Free Society*, Washington, D.C.: U.S. Government Printing Office, 1967.

Price, R.R., "Mentally Disordered and Dangerous Persons under the Criminal Law," *Canadian Journal of Corrections*, 12, 1970, pp. 241-264.

Qualter, T.H., *Propaganda and Psychological Warfare*, New York: Random House, 1962.

Quinney, R., *The Social Reality of Crime*, Boston: Little, Brown, 1970.

Ramsoy, N.R. (Rogoff), "On the flow of Talent in Society," *Acta Sociologica*, 9, 1965, pp. 152-174.

Record, W., "Some Reflections on Bureaucratic Trends in Sociological Research," *American Sociological Review*, 25, 1960, pp. 411-414.

Reissman, L., "The Solution Cycle of Social Problems," *American Sociologist*, 7, February, 1972, pp. 7-9.

Reynolds, L.T. and J.M. Reynolds, eds., *The Sociology of Sociology*, New York: McKay, 1970.

Richman, A., *Psychiatric Care in Canada: Extent and Results*, Royal Commission on Health Services, Ottawa: Queen's Printer, 1966.

Rinehart, J.W., *The Tyranny of Work*, Toronto: Academic Press Canada, 1975.

Rocher, G., *A General Introduction to Sociology: A Theoretical Perspective*, Toronto: Macmillan, 1972.

Roebuck, J. and S.C. Weeber, *Political Crime in the United States: Analyzing Crime By and Against Government*, New York: Praeger, 1978.

Rose, A.M., "History and Sociology of the Study of Social Problems," in *Handbook on the Study of Social Problems*, edited by E.O. Smigel, Chicago: Rand McNally, 1971.

Rosenhan, D.L., "On Being Sane in Insane Places," *Science*, 179, 1973, pp. 250-258.

Ross, R. and G.L. Staines, "The Politics of Analyzing Social Problems," *Social Problems*, 20, 1972.

Rossides, D.W., *Society as a Functional Process: An Introduction to Sociology*, Toronto: McGraw-Hill of Canada, 1968.

Rothman, D.J., *The Discovery of the Asylum*, Boston: Little, Brown, 1971.

Rubington, E. and M. Weinberg, eds., *The Study of Social Problems: Five Perspectives*, New York: Oxford University Press, 1971.

Rushing, W.A., "Status Resources, Societal Reactions, and Hospital Admission," *American Sociological Review*, 43, 1978, pp. 521-533.

Rutherford, P., *The Making of the Canadian Media*, Toronto: McGraw-Hill Ryerson, 1978.

Ryan, W., *Blaming the Victim*, New York: Vintage Books, 1971.

Sagarin, E., *Deviants and Deviance*, New York: Praeger, 1975.

Saint-Pierre, A., *Le Problème Social*, Montreal: Bibliothèque Canadienne, 1925.

Saint-Pierre, A., *Questions et Oeuvres Sociales Chez Nous*, Montreal: Ecole Sociale Populaire, 1914.

Sarbin, T., R. Taft, and D.E. Bailey, *Clinical Inference and Cognitive Theory*, New York: Holt, 1960.

Scheff, T., *Being Mentally Ill*, Chicago: Aldine, 1966.

Schiffer, M.E., "Fitness to Stand Trial," *University of Toronto Faculty of Law Review*, 35, 1977, pp. 1-25.

Schindeler, F. and C.M. Lanphier, "Social Science Research and Participatory Democracy in Canada," reprinted in *Social and Cultural Change in Canada*, edited by W.E. Mann, Toronto: Copp Clark, vol. 2, 1970, pp. 64-87.

Schoenfeld, A.C., *et al.*, "Constructing a Social Problem: The Press and the Environment," *Social Problems*, 27, 1979, pp. 38-61.

Schur, E., *Crimes Without Victims*, Englewood Cliffs, N.J.: Prentice-Hall, 1965.

Schur, E.M., "Psychiatrists Under Attack, The Rebellious Dr. Szasz," *The Atlantic*, June, 1966, pp. 72-76.

Schur, E.M., "Reactions to Deviance: A Critical Assessment," *American Journal of Sociology*, 75, 1969, pp. 309-322.

Seeman, M., "The Intellectual and the Language of the Minorities," *American Journal of Sociology*, 64, 1958, pp. 25-35.

Sellin, T. and M. Wolfgang, *The Measurement of Delinquency*, New York: Wiley, 1964.

Senate of Canada, *Poverty in Canada*, Ottawa: Parliamentary Secretary, 1980.

Shaver, K.G., "Interpersonal and Social Consequences of Attribution," in *Contemporary Issues in Social Psychology*, Third Edition, edited by J.L. Brigham and L.S. Wrightsman, Monterey, Cal.: Brooks, Cole, 1977.

Sherman, L.W., "Three Models of Organizational Corruption in Agencies of Social Control," *Social Problems*, 27, 1980, pp. 478-488.

Shibutani, T., *Society and Personality*, Englewood Cliffs, N.J.: Prentice-Hall, 1961.

Silverman, R.A. and J.J. Teevan, Jr., eds., *Crime in Canadian Society*, second edition, Toronto: Butterworths, 1980.

Simon, J.J., "Resources, Population, Environment: An Oversupply of False Bad News," *Science*, 208, June 27, 1980, pp. 1431-1437.

Singer, B.D., "American Invasion of the Mass Media in Canada," in *Critical Issues in Canadian Society*, edited by C.L. Boydell et al., Toronto: Holt, Rinehart and Winston of Canada, 1971, pp. 423-436.

Smoking and Health, Report of the Advisory Committee to the Surgeon General, Washington, D.C.: U.S. Government Printing Office, 1964.

Solomon, R. and T. Madison, "The Evolution of Non-Medical Opiate Use in Canada, 1870-1929," *Drug Forum*, 5, 1977, pp. 239-249.

Sorokin, P., *Contemporary Sociological Theories*, New York: Harper, 1928.

Spector, M. and J. Kitsuse, *Constructing Social Problems*, Menlo Park, Cal.: Benjamin/Cummings, 1977.

Srole, L., *et al., Mental Health in the Metropolis: The Midtown Manhattan Study*, New York: McGraw-Hill, 1962.

Steadman, H.J., "The Psychiatrist as a Conservative Agent of Social Control," *Social Problems*, 20, 1972, pp. 263-271.

Stuckey, W.K., "The Prize," *Saturday Review*, September 2, 1972, pp. 33-39.

Sumner, W.G., *What Social Classes Owe to Each Other*, New York: Harper and Row, 1900.

Sutherland, E.H., "Differential Association: Theory and Fact," in *The Sutherland Papers*, edited by A. Cohen et al., Bloomington: Indiana University Press, 1956, pp. 30-41.

Sutherland, E.H., "The Diffusion of Sexual Psychopath Laws," *American Journal of Sociology*, 56, 1950, pp. 142-148.

Sutherland, E.H., *Principles of Criminology*, Philadelphia: Lippincott, 1939.

Swadron, B., "The Unfairness of Unfitness," *Canadian Bar Review*, 9, 1966, pp. 76-77 and 113.

Sykes, G.M. and D. Matza, "Techniques of Neutralization: A Theory of Delinquency," *American Sociological Review*, 22, 1957, pp. 664-670.

Szasz, T.S., *Psychiatric Justice*, New York: Basic Books, 1966.

Szasz, T.S., *The Ethics of Psychoanalysis*, New York: Basic Books, 1965.

Szasz, T.S., *Law, Liberty and Psychiatry*, New York: Macmillan, 1963.

Szasz, T.S., *The Myth of Mental Illness*, New York: Hoeber-Harper, 1961.

Taber, M., *et al.*, "Disease Ideology and Mental Health Research," *Social Problems*, 16, 1969, pp. 349-357.

Taft, R., "The Ability to Judge People," *Psychological Bulletin*, 52, 1955, pp. 1-23.

Tallman, I. and R. McGee, "Definition of a Social Problem," in *Handbook on the Study of Social Problems*, edited by E.O. Smigel, Chicago: Rand McNally, 1971.

Tarsis, V., *Ward 7*, New York: Dutton, 1965.

Theodorson, G.A. and A.G. Theodorson, *A Modern Dictionary of Sociology*, New York: Crowell, 1969.

Thomas, W.I. and F. Znaniecki, *The Polish Peasant in Europe and America*, two-volume edition, New York: Dover, 1958 (first published in 1918).

Timlin, M.E. and A. Faucher, *The Social Sciences in Canada: Two Studies*, Ottawa: Social Science Research Council of Canada, 1968.

Tittle, C.R., "Deterrents or Labeling?" *Social Forces*, 53, 1975, pp. 399-410.

Toffler, A., *Future Shock*, New York: Bantam Books, 1970.

Trilling, L., *Beyond Culture*, New York: Viking Press, 1965.

Tuchman, G., *Making News: A Study in the Construction of Reality*, New York: Free Press, 1978.

Turner, R.H., "The Public Perception of Protest," *American Sociological Review*, 34, 1969, pp. 815-831.

Valaskakis, K., *et al.*, *The Conserver Society*, Don Mills, Ont.: Fitzhenry and Whiteside, 1979.

Vallee, F.G. and D.R. Whyte, "Canadian Society: Trends and Perspectives," in *Canadian Society: Sociological Perspectives*, abridged edition, edited by B.R. Blishen *et al.*, Toronto: Macmillan, 1968, pp. 556-575.

Vaz, E., *Aspects of Deviance*, Toronto: Prentice-Hall of Canada, 1976.

Vinet, A., "La vie quotidienne dans un asile Québécois," *Recherches Sociographiques*, 16, 1975, pp. 85-112.

Walker, N. and M. Argyle, "Does the Law Affect Moral Judgments?" *British Journal of Criminology*, 4, 1964, pp. 570-581.

Wallerstein, J.S. and J.B. Kelly, *Surviving the Breakup*, New York: Basic Books, 1980.

Watson, J.D., *The Double Helix*, New York: New American Library, 1969.

Webb, S. and B. Webb, *English Local Government: English Poor Law History, Part I.* New York: Longmans, Green, 1927.

Webb, S. and B. Webb, *English Poor Law History, Part I. The Old Poor Law*, Hamden, Conn.: Anchor Books, 1963.

White, D.M., "The Gate-Keeper: A Study of the Selection of News," in *People, Society, and Mass Communication*, edited by L.A. Dexter and D.M. White, New York: Free Press, 1968.

Willhelm, S.M., "Elites, Scholars, and Sociologists," *Catalyst*, 2, 1966, pp. 1-10.

Williams, J.I., *et al.*, "Mental Health and Illness in Canada," in *Deviant Behaviour and Societal Reaction*, edited by C.L. Boydell *et al.*, Toronto: Holt, Rinehart and Winston, 1972.

Williams, R.M., Jr., "Relative Deprivation," in *The Idea of Social Structure*, edited by L.A. Coser, New York: Harcourt Brace Jovanovich, 1975.

Wing, J.K., *Reasoning About Madness*, New York: Oxford University Press, 1978.

Wirth, L., "Ideological Aspects of Social Disorganization," *American Sociological Review*, 5, 1940, pp. 472-482.

Young, M., *The Rise of the Meritocracy*, New York: Random House, 1959.

INDEX

49354

Henshel, Richard L.

Perspectives on social
problems 2d ed. 1983